Learning ASP.NET Core MVC Programming

Learn the fundamentals of ASP.NET MVC and build
real-world web applications using ASP.NET Core MVC

Mugilan T. S. Ragupathi

BIRMINGHAM - MUMBAI

Learning ASP.NET Core MVC Programming

First published: November 2016

Production reference: 1101116

Published by Packt Publishing Ltd.
Livery Place
35 Livery Street
Birmingham
B3 2PB, UK.
ISBN 978-1-78646-383-8

www.packtpub.com

Credits

Author

Mugilan T. S. Ragupathi

Reviewers

Anuraj Parameswaran
Mustafa Erhan Ersoy
Anand Ranjan Pandey

Commissioning Editor

Edward Gordon

Acquisition Editor

Indrajit Das

Content Development Editor

Zeeyan Pinheiro

Technical Editor

Pavan Ramchandani

Copy Editor

Safis Editing

Project Coordinator

Suzanne Coutinho

Proofreader

Safis Editing

Indexer

Rekha Nair

Graphics

Kirk D'Penha

Production Coordinator

Melwyn D'sa

About the Author

Mugilan T. S. Ragupathi has been working on building web-based applications using Microsoft technology for more than a decade. He has been active in the ASP.NET community and has been running a successful blog, `www.dotnetodyssey.com` to help his fellow .NET developers.

His free beginners' course for ASP.NET MVC 5 (`http://www.dotnetodyssey.com/asp-net-mvc-5-free-course/`) was well received and is referred to as a concrete reference for beginners. He can be seen at csharp subreddit / Stack Overflow. He has written free micro eBooks, *The 7 Most Popular Recipes of jQuery with ASP.NET Web Forms* and *Value & Reference types in C#* (`http://www.dotnetodyssey.com/free-ebooks/`).

His book has received a good response and you can see the proof from one of his readers at `https://twitter.com/jeffadamez`. He is also an active contributor in Quora to the ASP.NET community (`https://www.quora.com/profile/Mugil-Ragu`). He likes to help readers with queries regarding ASP.NET.

About the Reviewers

Anuraj Parameswaran is a technical architect with Suyati Technologies (http://suyati.com/), Kochi. He has more than 12 years of extensive experience of working on different technologies, mostly in Microsoft space. He has been working on the .NET platform since its early days. He is a Microsoft Most Valuable Professional (MVP) in Visual Studio and Development Technologies. His focus areas are data analytics, architecture, and cloud computing. He is a K-MUG Community council member and an active volunteer in the Microsoft Technology Community. You can find his blog at http://dotnetthoughts.net.

Anuraj is also a reviewer of books and videos, namely, *ASP.NET Web API Security Essentials*, *Learning ASP.NET Web API*, and so on by Packt.

Mustafa Erhan Ersoy is a software team leader who is constantly evaluating new technologies and techniques in software development. He has been developing software professionally for 12 years and working mostly on ASP.NET web applications. He is very familiar with all aspects of transaction banking applications, BPM, and business workflows. He also blogs about web technologies, answers questions at stackoverflow.com, and participates in talks about ASP.NET and web technologies.

Anand Ranjan Pandey is currently working as a senior software developer for Dell. He is passionate about all aspects of software development, primarily and exclusively in the Microsoft .NET framework. He defines himself as an innovative technologist and visionary software developer with a passion for creating successful software products. He has comprehensive expertise in planning, managing, and achieving strategic business goals. Deep foundation in user-centered design, information architecture, and interactive new media.

He is an expert at building and leading cross-disciplinary technical teams and developing highly scalable and sustainable systems. He is successful at delivering technically challenging projects including enterprise e-commerce systems, secure exam portals, numerous software applications (web and shrink-wrap), content management systems, QA systems, networked publishing systems, and large-scale interactive multimedia learning exhibits.

www.PacktPub.com

For support files and downloads related to your book, please visit `www.PacktPub.com`.

Did you know that Packt offers eBook versions of every book published, with PDF and ePub files available? You can upgrade to the eBook version at `www.PacktPub.com` and as a print book customer, you are entitled to a discount on the eBook copy. Get in touch with us at `service@packtpub.com` for more details.

At `www.PacktPub.com`, you can also read a collection of free technical articles, sign up for a range of free newsletters and receive exclusive discounts and offers on Packt books and eBooks.

`https://www.packtpub.com/mapt`

Get the most in-demand software skills with Mapt. Mapt gives you full access to all Packt books and video courses, as well as industry-leading tools to help you plan your personal development and advance your career.

Why subscribe?

- Fully searchable across every book published by Packt
- Copy and paste, print, and bookmark content
- On demand and accessible via a web browser

Table of Contents

Preface

The book aims to help you learn the fundamentals of ASP.NET Core MVC and apply that knowledge to building applications using ASP.NET Core. This book also aims to serve as a solid guide for beginners who want to learn ASP.NET MVC. In detail, the following topics are going to be covered in the book:

- Fundamentals and objectives of ASP.NET Core MVC
- Philosophies (separation of concerns, convention over configuration) of ASP.NET Core
- Components of ASP.NET Core MVC—Controllers, Models, and Views
- Interacting with the database using Entity Framework
- Validating the user's input, both at the client-side and the server-side
- Provide a face-lift to the application using Bootstrap
- Making use of different deployment options provided by ASP.NET Core MVC

What this book covers

Chapter 1, Introduction to ASP.NET Core, covers the fundamentals of ASP.NET MVC and how it fits in the ASP.NET ecosystem. This chapter explains the basics of web development, including client-side components and server-side components and what a programmer can do and can't do in either layer

Chapter 2, Setting up the Environment, shows the reader how to set up the development environment, including the installation of Visual Studio and ASP.NET Core. Hardware and software requirements for setting up the development environment is also discussed and the anatomy of ASP.NET MVC applications is presented.

Chapter 3, Controllers, explains about what constitutes a Controller and action method along with its roles and responsibilities. In this chapter, a simple Controller along with an action method will be created. It will explain to the readers what an action method and a Controller does from the perspective of an overall ASP.NET MVC application.

Chapter 4, Views, presents what the Razor View engine does and explains the various basic programming constructs (conditionals, loops, and so on) with the examples using Razor view engine.

Chapter 5, Models, presents the role of Models in ASP.NET Core application. The concept of ViewModel is discussed along with how it provides flexibility and data compartmentalization to your applications.

Chapter 6, Validation, explains client-side and server-side validation with JavaScript and by using the jQuery libraries.

Chapter 7, Routing, explains about the routing module, which selects the appropriate controller from the received request with an example. Various options and features of routing are presented. This chapter will also guide you through building a custom route for ASP.NET MVC application based on business logic or for SEO purposes.

Chapter 8, Beautifying ASP.NET Application with Bootstrap, teaches how to use Bootstrap, a responsive frontend framework, to prettify your applications. You will be guided through the creation of HTML form controls.

Chapter 9, Deployment of ASP.NET Core Application, explains how the project.json library handles all of the dependencies of ASP.NET Core applications, along with the versions. It also explains how the K runtime (the latest option in ASP.NET Core application) so that an ASP.NET MVC application could be deployed in a non-Windows environment as well.

Chapter 10, Building Web Services Using Web API, explains HTTP-based services and how to implement them using the Web API. It will also introduce you to the Fiddler, and to compose an HTTP request using it.

Chapter 11, Improving Performance of an ASP.NET Core Application, explains the approaches to analyzing of performance and measures for improvement in various layers of your application.

Chapter 12, ASP.NET Core Identity, explains the security aspects of your application and implementing security identity of an application using Entity Framework.

What you need for this book

To start programming the ASP.NET MVC applications, you will need Visual Studio Community 2015 IDE. This is a fully featured IDE available for building desktops and web applications. You will also need various packages and frameworks, such as NuGet, Bootstrap, and project.json, the installation and configuration of which will be explained in the book.

Who this book is for

This book is for developers who want to learn how to build web applications using ASP.NET Core, developers who want to make a career building web applications using Microsoft technology, and developers who are working in Ruby on Rails or other web frameworks and want to learn how to use ASP.NET Core MVC.

No knowledge of the ASP.NET platform or the .NET platform is required. Even though you do not need to have experience with C#, an understanding of the basic constructs (loops, conditionals, classes, and objects) of any modern programming language would be helpful.

Conventions

In this book, you will find a number of text styles that distinguish between different kinds of information. Here are some examples of these styles and an explanation of their meaning.

Code words in text, database table names, folder names, filenames, file extensions, path names, dummy URLs, user input, and Twitter handles are shown as follows: "We need to add the `Kestrel HTTP Server` package as a dependency in the `project.json` framework"

A block of code is set as follows:

```
public static void Main(string[] args)
{
var host = new WebHostBuilder()
.UseKestrel()
}
```

Any command-line input or output is written as follows:

```
vi project.json
```

New terms and **important words** are shown in bold. Words that you see on the screen, for example, in menus or dialog boxes, appear in the text like this: "The shortcuts in this book are based on the `Mac OS X 10.5+` scheme."

Warnings or important notes appear in a box like this.

Tips and tricks appear like this.

Reader feedback

Feedback from our readers is always welcome. Let us know what you think about this book-what you liked or disliked. Reader feedback is important for us as it helps us develop titles that you will really get the most out of. To send us general feedback, simply e-mail `feedback@packtpub.com`, and mention the book's title in the subject of your message. If there is a topic that you have expertise in and you are interested in either writing or contributing to a book, see our author guide at `www.packtpub.com/authors`.

Customer support

Now that you are the proud owner of a Packt book, we have a number of things to help you to get the most from your purchase.

Downloading the example code

You can download the example code files for this book from your account at `http://www.packtpub.com`. If you purchased this book elsewhere, you can visit `http://www.packtpub.com/support` and register to have the files e-mailed directly to you.

You can download the code files by following these steps:

1. Log in or register to our website using your e-mail address and password.
2. Hover the mouse pointer on the **SUPPORT** tab at the top.
3. Click on **Code Downloads & Errata**.
4. Enter the name of the book in the **Search** box.

5. Select the book for which you're looking to download the code files.
6. Choose from the drop-down menu where you purchased this book from.
7. Click on **Code Download**.

Once the file is downloaded, please make sure that you unzip or extract the folder using the latest version of:

- WinRAR / 7-Zip for Windows
- Zipeg / iZip / UnRarX for Mac
- 7-Zip / PeaZip for Linux

The code bundle for the book is also hosted on GitHub at `https://github.com/PacktPubl ishing/learning-asp-dot-net-core-programming` . We also have other code bundles from our rich catalog of books and videos available at `https://github.com/PacktPublish ing/`. Check them out!

Downloading the color images of this book

We also provide you with a PDF file that has color images of the screenshots/diagrams used in this book. The color images will help you better understand the changes in the output. You can download this file from `http://www.packtpub.com/sites/default/files/downl oads/LearningAspDotNetCoreProgramming_ColorImages.pdf`.

Errata

Although we have taken every care to ensure the accuracy of our content, mistakes do happen. If you find a mistake in one of our books-maybe a mistake in the text or the code-we would be grateful if you could report this to us. By doing so, you can save other readers from frustration and help us improve subsequent versions of this book. If you find any errata, please report them by visiting `http://www.packtpub.com/submit-errata`, selecting your book, clicking on the **Errata Submission Form** link, and entering the details of your errata. Once your errata are verified, your submission will be accepted and the errata will be uploaded to our website or added to any list of existing errata under the Errata section of that title.

To view the previously submitted errata, go to `https://www.packtpub.com/books/conten t/support` and enter the name of the book in the search field. The required information will appear under the **Errata** section.

Piracy

Piracy of copyrighted material on the Internet is an ongoing problem across all media. At Packt, we take the protection of our copyright and licenses very seriously. If you come across any illegal copies of our works in any form on the Internet, please provide us with the location address or website name immediately so that we can pursue a remedy.

Please contact us at `copyright@packtpub.com` with a link to the suspected pirated material.

We appreciate your help in protecting our authors and our ability to bring you valuable content.

Questions

If you have a problem with any aspect of this book, you can contact us at `questions@packtpub.com`, and we will do our best to address the problem.

1
Introduction to ASP.NET Core

ASP.NET Core, the latest version of ASP.NET MVC from Microsoft, is the server-side web application development framework which helps you to build web applications effectively. This runs on top of the ASP.NET 5 platform, which enables your application to be run on a wide variety of platforms, including Linux and Mac OS X. This opens up heaps of opportunities and it is exciting to be a .NET developer in these times.

In this chapter, you'll learn about the following topics:

- Fundamental concepts about web applications—HTTP, client-side, and server-side
- Three programming models of ASP.NET—ASP.NET Web Forms, ASP.NET Web Pages, and ASP.NET MVC
- Philosophy of ASP.NET MVC
- Features of ASP.NET Core and ASP.NET 5

Before discussing the ASP.NET Core and its features, let us understand the fundamentals of web applications development. I strongly believe the principle that if you want to be an expert at something, you need to be very good at the fundamentals. It will be helpful in debugging the issues and fixing them.

Having said that we are going to discuss the following key fundamentals:

- How web applications work, and a bit about HTTP
- Client-side and server-side
- HTTP methods

Just three key concepts. No big deal!

How web applications work

All web applications, irrespective of whether they are built using ASP.NET MVC, Ruby on Rails, or any other new shiny technology, work on the HTTP protocol. Some applications use HTTPS (a secure version of HTTP), where data is encrypted before passing through the wire. But HTTPS still uses HTTP.

So what is an HTTP protocol?

HTTP stands for **Hyper Text Transfer Protocol** and is an application protocol which is designed for distributed hypermedia systems. "Hyper Text" in Hyper Text Transfer Protocol refers to the structured text that uses hyperlinks for traversing between the documents. Standards for HTTP were developed by the **Internet Engineering Task Force (IETF)** and the **World Wide Web Consortium(W3C)**. The current version of HTTP is HTTP/2 and was standardized in 2015. It is supported by the majority of web browsers, such as Internet Explorer, Chrome, and Firefox.

The HTTP protocol (a protocol is nothing but a set of rules which govern the communication) is a stateless protocol that follows the request-response pattern.

Request-response pattern

Before talking about the request-response pattern, let us discuss a couple of terms: Client and server. A server is a computing resource that receives the requests from the clients and serves them. A server, typically, is a high-powered machine with huge memory to process many requests. A client is a computing resource that sends a request and receives the response. A client, typically, could be a web server or any application that sends the requests.

Coming back to the request-response pattern, when you request a resource from a server, the server responds to you with the requested resource. A resource could be anything—a web page, text file, an image , or another data format.

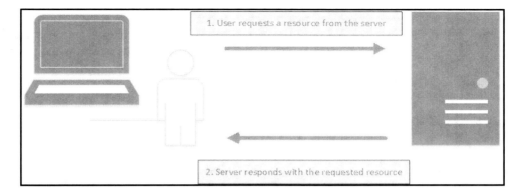

You fire a request. The server responds with the resource. This is called a **request-response pattern**.

Stateless nature of HTTP

When you request for the same resource again, the server responds to you with the requested resource again without having any knowledge of the fact that the same was requested and served earlier. The HTTP protocol inherently does not have any knowledge of the state knowledge of any of the previous requests received and served. There are several mechanisms available that maintain the state, but the HTTP protocol by itself does not maintain the state. We will explain the mechanisms to maintain the state later.

Let me explain to you about the statelessness and the request-response pattern to you with a simple practical example:

1. You type the following URL: https://en.wikipedia.org/wiki/ASP.NET_MVC. This is a Wikipedia web page about ASP.NET MVC.
2. From the preceding URL, the browser fires a request to the Wikipedia server.
3. The web server at Wikipedia serves you the ASP.NET MVC web page.
4. Your browser receives that web page and presents it.
5. You request the same page again by typing the same URL again (https://en.wikipedia.org/wiki/ASP.NET_MVC) and press *Enter*.
6. The browser again fires the request to the Wikipedia server.
7. Wikipedia serves you the same ASP.NET MVC web page without being aware of the fact that the same resource was requested previously from the same resource.

As mentioned earlier, there are several mechanisms to maintain the state. Let us assume, for the time being, that no such mechanism is implemented here. I know that I am being too simplistic here, but this explains the point.

Client-side and server-side

It is necessary to understand the client-side and server-side of web applications and what can be done either side. With respect to web applications, your client is the browser and your server could be the web server/application server.

The browser side is whatever that happens in your browser. It is the place where your JavaScript code runs and your HTML elements reside.

The server-side is whatever happens at the server at the other end of your computer. The request that you fire from your browser has to travel through the wire (probably across the network) to execute some server-side code and returns the appropriate response. Your browser is oblivious to the server-side technology or the language your server-side code is written in. The server-side is also the place where your C# code resides.

Let us discuss some of the facts to make things clear:

- **Fact 1**: All browsers can only understand HTML, CSS, and JavaScript, irrespective of the browser vendor.
  - You might be using Internet Explorer, Firefox, Chrome, or any other browser. Still, the fact that your browser can understand only HTML, CSS, and JavaScript holds true. It cannot understand C#. It cannot understand Java. Nor Ruby. Only HTML, CSS, and JavaScript. This is the reason why you can access the web applications, built using any technology could be accessed by the same browser.

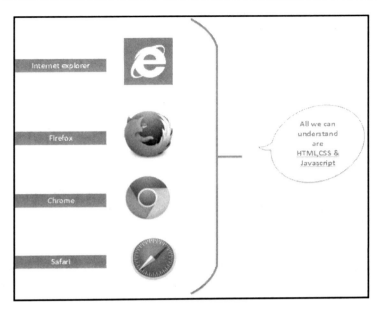

- **Fact 2**: The purpose of any web development framework is to convert your server-side code to HTML, CSS, and JavaScript.
  - This is related to the previous point. As browsers can only understand HTML, CSS, and JavaScript, all the web development technologies should convert your server-side code to HTML, CSS, and JavaScript so that your browser can understand. This is the primary purpose of any web development framework. This is true for whether you build your web applications using ASP.NET MVC, ASP.NET Web Forms, Ruby on Rails, or J2EE. Each web development framework may have a unique concept/implementation regarding how to generate the HTML, CSS, and JavaScript, and may handle features such as security performance differently. But still, each framework has to produce the HTML, because that's what your browsers understand.

HTTP methods

Even though all the requests of the HTTP protocol follow the request-response pattern, the way the requests are sent can vary from one to the next. The HTTP method defines how the request is being sent to the server.

The available methods in HTTP are GET, HEAD, POST, PUT, DELETE, TRACE, OPTIONS, CONNECT, and PATCH. In most of the web applications, the GET and POST methods are widely used. In this section, we will discuss these methods. Later, we will discuss other HTTP methods on a need-to-know basis.

GET method

GET is a method of the HTTP protocol which is used to get a resource from the server. Requests which use the GET method should only retrieve the data and should not have any side effect. This means that if you fire the same GET request, again and again, you should get the same data, and there should not be any change in the state of the server, as a result of this GET request.

In the GET method, the parameters are sent as part of the request URL and therefore will be visible to the end user. The advantage of this approach is that the user can bookmark the URL and visit the page again whenever they want. An example is www.yourwebsite.com?tech=mvc6&db=sql.

We are passing a couple of parameters in the preceding GET request. tech is the first parameter with the value mvc6 and db is the second parameter with the value sql. Assume your website takes the preceding parameters with values and searches in your database to retrieve the blog posts that talk about mvc6 and sql before presenting those blog posts to the user.

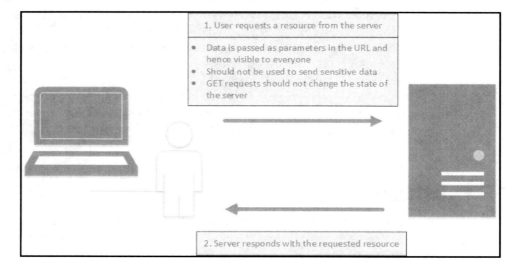

The disadvantage of the GET method is that, as the data is passed in clear text in the URL as parameters, it cannot be used to send the sensitive information.

Moreover, most browsers have limitations on the number of characters in the URL, so, when using GET requests, we cannot send large amounts of data.

POST method

The POST request is generally used to update or create resources at the server.

Data is passed in the body of the request. This has the following implications:

- You can send sensitive information to the server, as the data is embedded in the body of the request and it will not be visible to the end user in the URL.
- As the data is not sent through the request URL, it does not take up space in the URL and therefore it has no issues with the URL length limitations.

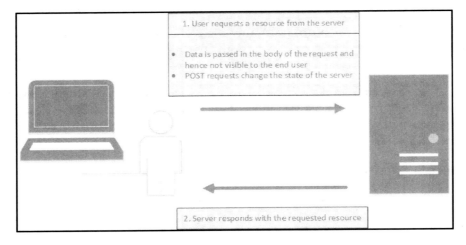

As we have covered the fundamentals, we can now proceed to discuss ASP.NET.

What is ASP.NET?

ASP.NET is a server-side web application development framework allowing developers to build web applications, websites, and web services. It was first introduced by Microsoft in early 2002, and in these 14 years, it has undergone a lot of changes.

Basically, ASP.NET has three programming models:

- ASP.NET Web Forms
- ASP.NET Web Pages
- ASP.NET MVC

Even though the end result of all of the preceding programming models is to produce the dynamic web pages effectively, the methodologies that they follow differ from each other. Let us discuss each one of these programming models to understand their principles.

ASP.NET Web Forms

Historically, when ASP.NET was first introduced, ASP.NET Web Forms was the only programming model available to programmers to develop web applications in ASP.NET.

The ASP.NET Web Forms model abstracted the web so that it can maintain the state even though the web is inherently stateless.

It also supports the event-driven programming model at the server-side. This has helped desktop application developers to have a smooth transition in moving into web application development.

Like PHP and several other web application frameworks, ASP.NET Web Forms is a file-based framework where users access the web page by means of accessing a file at the server. The server will process your request, convert all of your server-side components in that file to HTML, and send it back to the requesting client.

Each web page in ASP.NET Web Forms is represented by two files: `.aspx` and `.aspx.cs` or `.aspx.vb`. The `.aspx` file contains your front end components-all of your ASP controls and your HTML elements. The `.aspx.cs` (if you are using C# as the code-behind language) or `.aspx.vb` (if you are using Visual Basic as the code-behind programming language) contains the code for events which are happening at the web page.

This was the predominant programming model prior to the arrival of ASP.NET MVC, and this programming model is still being used to maintain the production applications that were written using this model.

ASP.NET Web Pages

ASP.NET Web Pages are primarily targeted at small web applications where the data-processing logic is written directly on the web page.

ASP.NET MVC

ASP.NET MVC is the implementation of the MVC pattern in ASP.NET. The disadvantages of ASP.NET Web Forms, such as limited control over the generation of HTML are resolved in ASP.NET MVC. As most of the modern applications are controlled by client-side JavaScript libraries/frameworks, such as **jQuery**, **KnockoutJS**, and **AngularJS**, having complete control over the generated HTML is of paramount importance.

Let us talk a bit about the Model-View-Controller pattern and how it benefits the web application development.

Model-View-Controller (MVC) pattern: This is a software architectural pattern which helps in defining the responsibility for each of the components and how they fit together in achieving the overall goal. This pattern is primarily used in building user interfaces, and is applicable in many areas including developing desktop applications and web applications. But I am going to explain the MVC pattern from the context of web development.

Primarily, the MVC pattern has three components:

- **Model**: This component represents your domain data. Please note that this is not your database. This model component can talk to your database, but the model only represents your domain data. For example, if you are building an e-commerce web application, the model component may contain classes such as Product, Supplier, and Inventory.
- **View**: This component is responsible for what to present to the user. Usually, this component would contain your HTML and CSS files. This may also include the layout information governing how your web application looks to the end user.

- **Controller**: As the name implies, the controller is responsible for interacting with different components. It receives the request (through the routing module), talks to the model, and sends the appropriate view to the user.

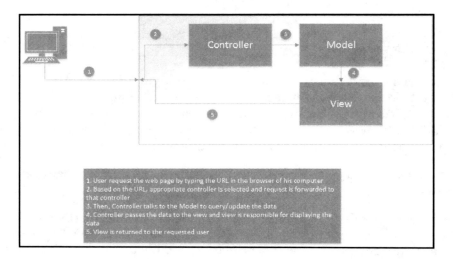

This separation of responsibilities brings great flexibility to the web application development, allowing each area to be managed separately and independently.

Features of ASP.NET MVC

ASP.NET MVC is an opinionated application development framework that prefers some functionality to be handled in a certain unique way. Let us discuss each of the features of ASP.NET MVC, along with the benefits they bring to the table.

Convention over configuration

This is a design methodology that significantly reduces the number of decisions while developing the application, and thus making it simpler.

If you have built any application using any technology, you might be using some kind of XML file where you have to configure everything in it. Even for the simpler straightforward things, we might have to configure the things over there.

ASP.NET MVC embraces *convention over configuration* completely. It is the philosophy where you can be certain of how it is going to work without ever configuring same.

Let me give you a simple example. All Controller code resides in the `Controller` folder, and Views have a separate folder for each of the Controllers. Whenever a request comes, ASP.NET MVC knows where to find the Controller and its associated View without any configuration. This methodology results in less configuration and less time in debugging.

Separation of concerns

As discussed earlier, ASP.NET MVC has three major components—Model, Controller, and Views. This clearly separates the responsibilities so that the UI designer or UI developer can work on the View while backend developers can work on the Model to build a data domain for the application or to talk to the database. As the duties of each of the components are clearly defined and separated, the work can be done in parallel.

Control over the generated HTML

If you have any experience in building an ASP.NET Web Forms application, you might have used ASP controls such as `asp:textbox`. Even though these controls have a lot of benefits, they have their cons as well. Developers cannot have complete control over the generated HTML when using these controls. Of course, you can set some properties in ASP control which in turn set some attributes in your generated HTML. But complete control is not possible. ASP.NET MVC HTML helpers and Tag helpers in ASP.NET Core provide better control over the generated HTML.

Better support for unit testing

As each of the components is separated and compartmentalized, creating the unit test cases becomes easier to achieve:

- **Unified MVC and Web API Controller in ASP.NET Core**: In earlier versions of ASP.NET MVC, different controllers were used for MVC (`System.Web.MVC.Controller`) and Web API (`System.Web.Http.ApiController`). In ASP.NET Core, there is only one base controller that supports creating both MVC controllers and Web API controllers. With respect to routing, all the controllers use the same routes. Of course, you can use convention-based routing or attribute-based routing depending on your needs.

- **Note about Web API**: Web API is the Microsoft technology for building web services over the HTTP protocol. HTTP is not only limited to serving web pages. Web API could be used for building API services and data. The advantage of this approach is that the services which are built using Web API could be consumed by a wide range of clients such as, browsers, mobile applications, and desktop applications.

The code for the earlier version of ASP.NET MVC (till ASP.NET MVC 5) is as follows:

```
publicclassValuesController : ApiController
{
  // GET api/values
  publicIEnumerable<string>Get()
  {
    returnnewstring[] { "value1","value2"};
  }
}
Code for ASP.NET Core:
publicclassValuesController:Controller
{
  //GET api/values
  [HttpGet]
  publicIEnumerable<string>Get()
  {
    returnnewstring[] { "value1","value2"};
  }
}
```

ASP.NET 5

ASP.NET 5 is the latest framework from Microsoft for building modern cloud-based applications using .NET. It is a cross-platform framework so that you can run your applications built on ASP.NET 5 on any platform, such as Linux or Mac OS X and also on Microsoft Windows, obviously. ASP.NET 5 is open source, and the complete source code is available on GitHub at `https://github.com/aspnet/home`.

The latest version of ASP.NET MVC, ASP.NET Core—runs on the ASP.NET 5 platform.

Features of ASP.NET 5

- **Cross-platform support**: Applications that are built on top of ASP.NET 5 can run on any platform where ASP.NET 5 is installed. This means that the applications that you build on ASP.NET 5 can run on Apple OS X and Linux machines. Deploying ASP.NET Core on a Linux machine will be explained in a later chapter.
- **Better support for client-side development**: ASP.NET 5 is designed to work seamlessly with a range of client-side frameworks, such as **AngularJs**, **Knockout**, **Bootstrap**, and **React.js**.

Summary

In this chapter, we have learned the basics of web development, including what constitutes the server-side and client-side. We have even discussed the features of ASP.NET Core and ASP.NET 5.

2

Setting Up the Environment

In any development project, it is vital to set up the right kind of development environment so that you can concentrate on the developing the solution rather than solving environment issues or configuration problems. With respect to .NET, Visual Studio is the defacto standard **IDE (Integrated Development Environment)** for building web applications in .NET.

In this chapter, you'll be learning about the following topics:

- Purpose of IDE
- Different offerings of Visual Studio
- Installation of Visual Studio Community 2015
- Creating your first ASP.NET MVC 5 project and project structure

Purpose of IDE

First of all, let us see why we need an IDE, when you can type the code in Notepad, compile it, and execute it.

When you develop a web application, you might need the following things to be productive:

- **Code editor**: This is the text editor where you type your code. Your code editor should be able to recognize different constructs such as the `if` condition, `for` loop of your programming language. In Visual Studio, all of your keywords would be highlighted in blue color.

- **Intellisense**: Intellisense is a context aware code-completion feature available in most modern IDEs including Visual Studio. One such example is when you type a dot after an object; this *Intellisense* feature lists out all the methods available on the object. This helps the developers to write code faster and easier.
- **Build/Publish**: It would be helpful if you could build or publish the application using a single click or single command. Visual Studio provides several options out-of-the-box to build a separate project or to build the complete solution in a single click. This makes the build and deployment of your application easier.
- **Templates**: Depending on the type of the application, you might have to create different folders and files along with the boilerplate code. So, it'll be very helpful if your IDE supports the creation of different kinds of template. Visual Studio generates different kinds of templates with the code for ASP.NET Web Forms, MVC, and Web API to get you up-and-running.
- **Ease of adding items**: Your IDE should allow you to add different kinds of items with ease. For example, you should be able to add an XML file without any issues. And if there is any problem with the structure of your XML file, it should be able to highlight the issue and provide information to help you to fix the issues.

Visual Studio offerings

There are different versions of Visual Studio 2015 available to satisfy the various needs of developers/organizations. Primarily, there are four versions of Visual Studio 2015:

- **Visual Studio Community**
- **Visual Studio Professional**
- **Visual Studio Enterprise**
- **Visual Studio Test Professional**

System requirements

Visual Studio can be installed on computers running Windows 7 Service Pack 1 operating system and above. You can get to know the complete list of requirements from the following URL:

```
https://www.visualstudio.com/en-us/downloads/visual-studio-2015-system-requi
rements-vs.aspx
```

Visual Studio Community 2015

This is a fully featured IDE available for building desktops, web applications, and cloud services. It is available free of cost for individual users.

You can download Visual Studio Community from the following URL:

```
https://www.visualstudio.com/en-us/products/visual-studio-community-vs.aspx
```

Throughout this book, we will be using the Visual Studio Community version for development as it is available free of cost to individual developers.

Visual Studio Professional

As the name implies, Visual Studio Professional is targeted at professional developers and contains features such as **Code Lens** for improving your team's productivity. It also has features for greater collaboration within the team.

Visual Studio Enterprise

Visual Studio Enterprise is the full-blown version of Visual Studio with a complete set of features for collaboration, including a team foundation server, modeling, and testing.

Visual Studio Test Professional

Visual Studio Test Professional is primarily aimed for the testing team or people who are involved in the testing, which might include developers. In any software development methodology, either the waterfall model or agile developers need to execute the development suite test cases for the code they are developing.

Installing Visual Studio Community

Follow the given steps to install Visual Studio Community 2015:

1. Visit the following link to download Visual Studio Community 2015:

`https://www.visualstudio.com/en-us/products/visual-studio-community-vs.aspx`

2. Click on the **Download Community 2015** button. Save the file in a folder where you can retrieve it easily later:

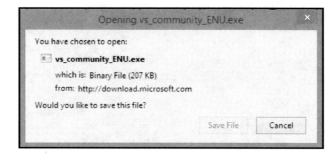

3. Run the downloaded executable file:

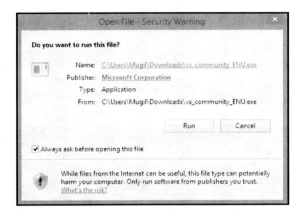

4. Click on **Run** and the following screen will appear:

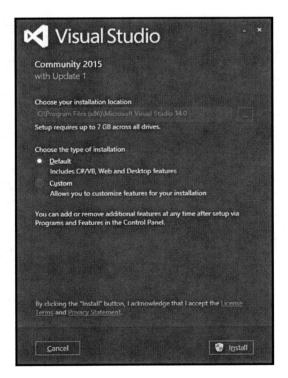

There are two types of installation—default and custom installation. The default installation installs the most commonly used features and this will cover most developer use cases of the developer. Custom installation helps you to customize the components that you want to install:

1. Click on the **Install** button after selecting the installation type.
2. Depending on your memory and processor speed, the installation will take 1 to 2 hours to install.

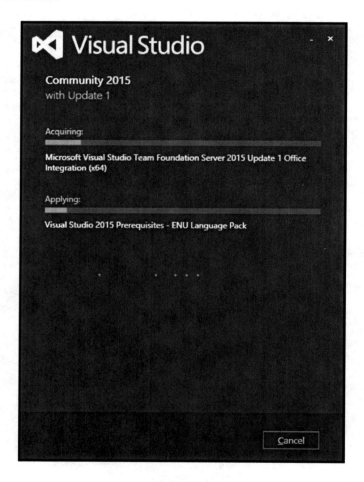

3. Once all the components are installed, you will see the following **Setup Completed** screen:

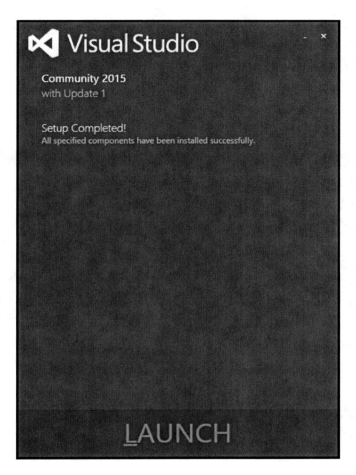

Installing ASP.NET 5

When we install the Visual Studio Community 2015 edition, ASP.NET 5 will be installed by default. As the ASP.NET Core application runs on top of ASP.NET 5, we need to install ASP.NET 5.

There are a couple of ways to install ASP.NET 5:

- Get ASP.NET 5 from `https://get.asp.net/`

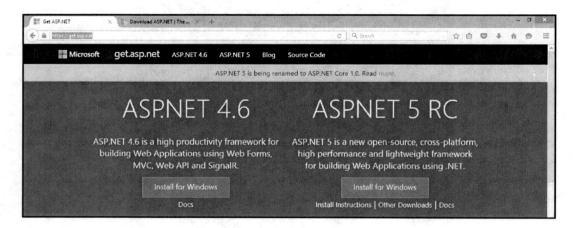

- Another option is to install from the **New Project** template in Visual Studio

This option is a bit easier as you don't need to search and install.

The following are the detailed steps:

1. Create a new project by selecting **File** | **New** | **Project** or using the shortcut *Ctrl + Shift + N*:

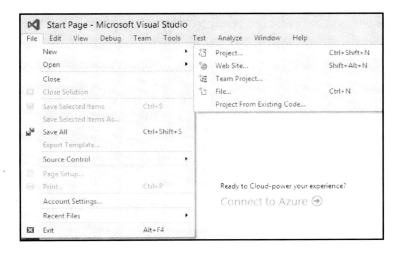

2. Select **ASP.NET Web Application** and enter the project name and click on **OK**:

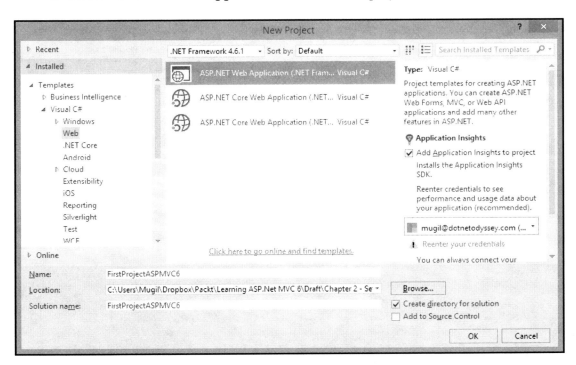

3. The following window will appear to select a template. Select the **Get ASP.NET 5 RC** option as shown in the following screenshot:

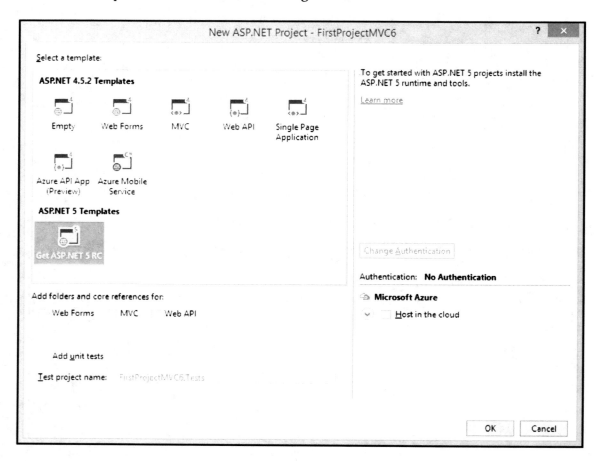

4. When you click on **OK** in the preceding screen, the following window will appear:

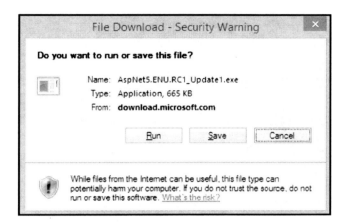

5. When you click on the **Run** or **Save** button in the preceding dialog, you will get the following screen asking for ASP.NET 5 Setup. Select the checkbox, **I agree to the license terms and conditions** and click on the **Install** button:

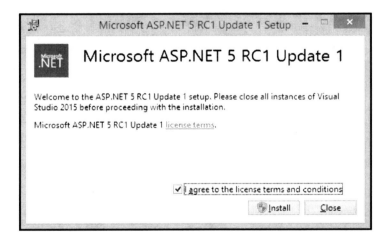

6. Installing of ASP.NET 5 might take a couple of hours. Once it is completed you'll get the following screen:

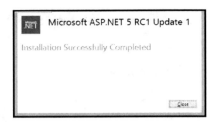

During the process of installing **ASP.NET 5 RC1 Update 1**, it might ask you to close the Visual Studio. If asked, please do so.

Project structure in ASP.NET 5 application

Once ASP.NET 5 RC1 is successfully installed, open the Visual Studio, create a new project and select the ASP.NET 5 **Web Application** as shown in the following screenshot:

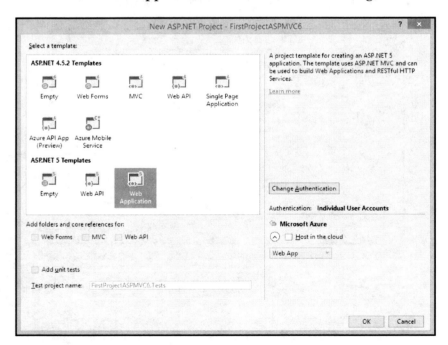

A new project will be created and the structure will be like following:

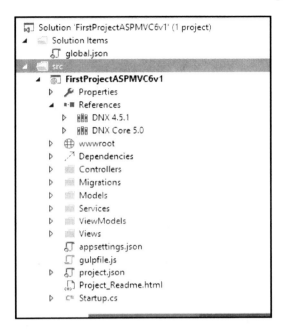

File-based project

Whenever you add a file or folder in your file system (inside the ASP.NET 5 project folder), the changes will be automatically reflected in your application.

Support for full .NET and .NET core

You might have noticed a couple of references in the preceding project: **DNX 4.5.1** and **DNX Core 5.0**. **DNX 4.5.1** provides functionalities of full-blown .NET whereas **DNX Core 5.0** supports only the core functionalities, which would be used if you are deploying the application across cross-platforms such as Apple OS X, Linux. The development and deployment of an ASP.NET Core application on a Linux machine will be explained in a later chapter.

The Project.json package

Usually, in an ASP.NET web application, we would have the assemblies as references and the list of references in a C# project file. But in an ASP.NET 5 application, we have a JSON file by name `Project.json`, which will contain all the necessary configurations with all its .NET dependencies in the form of `NuGet` packages. This makes dependency management easier. `NuGet` is a package manager, provided by Microsoft, which makes package installation and uninstallation easier. Prior to `NuGet`, all dependencies had to be installed manually. The dependencies section identifies the list of dependent packages available for the application. The frameworks section informs us about frameworks, supported by the application. The scripts section identifies the script to be executed during the build process of the application. Include and exclude properties can be used in any section to include or exclude any item.

Controllers

This folder contains all of your controller files. Controllers are responsible for handling requests, communicating models, and generating the views.

Models

All of your classes representing domain data will be present in this folder.

Views

Views are files that contain your frontend components and are presented to the end users of the application. This folder contains all of your **Razor** View files.

Migrations

Any database-related migrations will be available in this folder. Database migrations are the C# files which contain the history of any database changes done through an **Entity Framework** (an ORM framework). This will be explained in detail in a later chapter.

The wwwroot folder

This folder acts as a root folder and it is the ideal container to place all of your static files such as CSS and JavaScript files. All the files which are placed in wwwroot folder can be directly accessed from the path without going through the controller.

Other files

The appsettings.json file is the config file where you can configure application level settings. **Bower, npm (Node Package Manager)**, and **gulpfile.js** are client-side technologies, supported by ASP.NET 5 applications.

Summary

In this chapter, you learned about the offerings in Visual Studio. Step-by-step instructions are provided for installing the Visual Studio Community version, freely available for individual developers. We have also discussed the new project structure of the ASP.NET 5 application and the changes when compared to the previous versions.

In the next chapter, we are going to discuss the controllers and their roles and functionalities. We'll also build a controller and associated action methods and see how they work.

3
Controllers

As discussed in the first chapter, all web applications receive requests from the server and produce a response, that is delivered back to the end user. A Controller does the job of receiving the request and producing the output based on the input data in ASP.NET MVC.

In this chapter, you'll be learning about the following topics:

- Role of the Controller in ASP.NET MVC applications
- Routing introduction and concepts
- Creating your first ASP.NET 5 application
- Installation of the ASP.NET Core `NuGet` packages in your application
- Creation of your first Controller and `action` method, which returns a simple *Hello World*
- Adding a View and making the changes that allow your Controller to use that View
- Adding a Model and passing that Model data to your View

Role of the Controller in ASP.NET MVC applications

At the high level, the Controller orchestrates between the Model and the View, and sends the output back to the user. This is also the place where authentication is usually done through action filters. Action filters will be discussed in detail in the *Filters* section of this chapter. The following figure illustrates the high-level flow of a request (with the steps) in ASP.Net MVC and shows us how the Controller fits into the big picture:

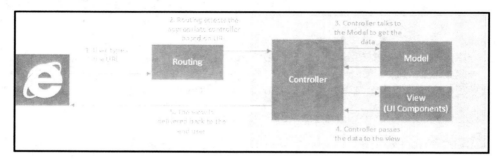

The following is the sequence of events that will happen at high level when the user is accessing the ASP.NET Core application:

1. The user types the URL in the browser.
2. Based on the pattern of the URL, the routing engine selects the appropriate Controller.
3. The Controller talks to the Model to get any relevant data through its action methods. Action methods are methods within a `controller` class.
4. The Controller then passes the data to the View to present it in a viewable format, typically as HTML elements.
5. The View is finally delivered to the user, which he would be viewing in his browser.

Before discussing the controller, let us discuss the fundamentals of routing concepts, as the routing engine only chooses the appropriate `controller` and `action` method at runtime.

Introduction to routing

The routing engine is responsible for getting the incoming request and routing that request to the appropriate Controller based on the URL pattern. We can configure the routing engine so that it can choose the appropriate controller based on the relevant information.

By convention, ASP.NET MVC follows this pattern: **Controller/Action/Id.**

If the user types the URL `http://yourwebsite.com/Hello/Greeting/1`, the routing engine selects the `Hello controller` class and `Greeting action` method within the `HelloController`, and passes the `Id` value as 1. You can give default values to some of the parameters and make some of the parameters optional.

The following is the sample configuration:

```
The template: "{controller=Hello}/{action=Greeting}/{id?}");
```

In the preceding configuration, we are giving three instructions to the routing engine:

- Use the routing pattern `controller/action/id`.
- Use the default values `Hello` and `Greeting` for the `controller` and `action` respectively, if the values for `controller` or `action` are not supplied in the URL.
- Make the `Id` parameter optional so that the URL does not need to have this information. If the URL contains this `Id` information, it will use it. Otherwise, the `Id` information will not be passed to the `action` method.

Let us discuss how the routing engine selects the `controller` classes, `action` methods, and `Id` values for different URLs:

```
URL1:http://localhost/
Controller: Hello
Action method: Greeting
Id: no value is passed for the id parameter
```

Reasoning: The `Hello` controller is passed as the default value as per the routing configuration, as no value is passed as the Controller in the URL.

The following action method will be picked up by the routing handler when the preceding URL is passed:

```
public class HelloController : Controller {
  public ActionResult Greeting(int id) {
    return View();
  }
}


URL2: http://localhost/Hello/Greeting2
Controller: Hello
Action method: Greeting2
Id: no value is passed for the id parameter
```

Reasoning: The Hello controller will be chosen as the URL contains Hello as the first parameter, and the Greeting2 action method will be chosen as the URL contains Greeting2 as the second parameter. Please note that the default value mentioned in the configuration would be picked only when no value is present in the URL. As the id parameter is optional and the URL does not contain the value for id, no value is passed to the id parameter.

The following action method Greeting2 will be picked up by the routing handler when the preceding URL is passed:

```
public class HelloController : Controller {
  public ActionResult Greeting(int id) {
    return View();
  }

  public ActionResult Greeting2(int id) {
    return View();
  }
}


URL3: http://localhost/Hello2/Greeting2
Controller: Hello2
Action method: Greeting2
Id: no value is passed for the id parameter
```

Reasoning: As `Hello2` is passed as the first parameter, the `Hello2` controller will be selected, and `Greeting2` is the action method selected since `Greeting2` is passed as the second parameter. As the `id` parameter is optional and no value is passed for the parameter `id`, no value will be passed for the `id`.

The following `action` method will be picked up by the routing handler when the preceding URL is passed:

```
public class Hello2Controller : Controller {
  public ActionResult Greeting2(int id) {
    return View();
  }
}
URL4: http://localhost/Hello3/Greeting2/1
Controller: Hello3
Action method: Greeting2
Id: 1
```

Reasoning: `Hello3` is the controller selected as it is mentioned as the first parameter, `Greeting4` is the action method, and `1` is the value passed as the `id`.

The following `action` method will be picked up the routing handler when the preceding URL is passed:

```
public class Hello3Controller : Controller {
  public ActionResult Greeting2(int id) {
    return View();
  }
}
```

We will discuss routing in detail in a later chapter.

Once the request reaches the controller, the controller will create a response by talking to the Model and may pass the data to View and the View will then be rendered to the end user.

Creating ASP.NET 5 application

It's time to get our hands dirty. Let us create a simple ASP.NET 5 application. Fire up Visual Studio and follow these steps:

1. Create a project by selecting **File** | **New Project** in Visual Studio. The first option is for creating an earlier version of the ASP.NET Web application. The second option is for creating the ASP.NET Core application using the .NET Core framework. The third option is for creating the ASP.NET Core application using the .NET framework. The difference between the second and third option is that the .NET framework supports all the functionalities of existing .NET frameworks whereas .NET Core supports only the core functionalities. The advantage of using the .NET core library is that it can be deployed on any platform.

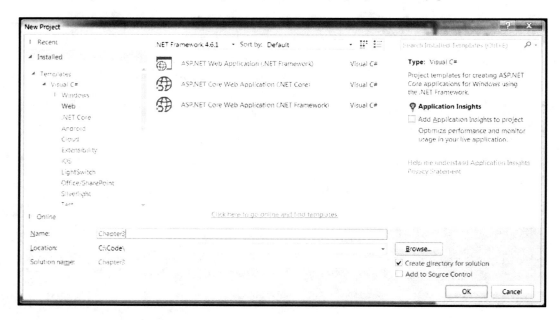

2. Select the **Empty** template from the list of ASP.NET 5 templates. The second option is for creating the Web API application (for building the HTTP-based services) and the third option is for creating a web application containing some basic functionalities which you can run just from out of the box without you ever needing to write anything.

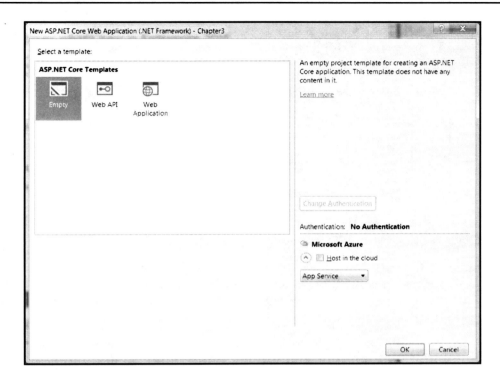

3. Once you click **OK** in the window as shown in the preceding screenshot, (after selecting the Empty template option) a solution will be created as shown in the following screenshot:

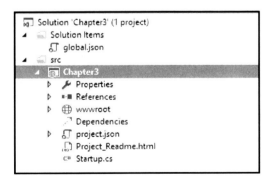

4. When you run the application (by pressing F5) without any changes, you'll get the simple **Hello World!** text on your screen as shown in the following screenshot:

We have not done any coding in this newly created application. So, have you thought about how it displays the text **Hello World!**?

The answer lies in the `Startup.cs` file, which contains a class by the name of `Startup`. This class contains the `Main` method, which acts as the entry point for the web application. If you have used any of the previous versions of ASP.NET MVC, or even ASP.NET Web Forms, this would not be the case.

ASP.NET 5 runtime calls the `ConfigureServices` and `Configure` methods. For example, if you want to configure any service, you can add it here. Any custom configuration for your application can be added to this `Configure` method:

```
public void ConfigureServices(IServiceCollection services) {

}

// This method gets called by the runtime. Use this method to  configure
the HTTP request pipeline.
public void Configure(IApplicationBuilder app) {
  app.UseIISPlatformHandler();
  app.Run(async (context) => {
    await context.Response.WriteAsync("Hello World!");
  });

}
```

There are only a couple of statements in the `Configure` method. The first statement tells the run-time to use the `IISPlatformHandler` for handling all the incoming HTTP requests. Let us leave aside `async`, `await`, and `context` for the moment in the second statement, which we will discuss later. In essence, the second statement tells the run-time to return `Hello World!` for all the incoming requests irrespective of the incoming URL.

When you type the URL `http://localhost:50140/Hello` in your browser, it will still return the same **Hello World!**.

This is the reason we got the **Hello World!** when we ran the application.

As we have chosen the **Empty** template while creating the ASP.NET 5 application, no component will have been installed. Even MVC wouldn't be installed by default when you select the **Empty** template as we did.

You can confirm it by opening the `project.json` file, where you can see no ASP.NET MVC is mentioned in the list of dependencies:

```
"dependencies": {
  "Microsoft.AspNet.IISPlatformHandler": "1.0.0-rc1-final",
  "Microsoft.AspNet.Server.Kestrel": "1.0.0-rc1-final"
},
```

So first, let us install the ASP.Net Core package for our application.

Installing the ASP.NET Core NuGet package in your application

Follow these steps to install the NuGet package of ASP.NET MVC:

1. Right click on the project, and select the **Manage NuGet Packages** option:

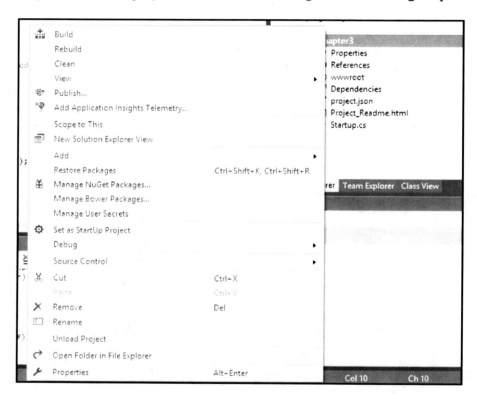

2. Select the **Include Prerelease** checkbox so that the **NuGet Package Manager** will list out all the prerelease packages. Search for MVC and you'll get the**Microsoft.AspNet.MVC** package, as shown in the following result, and click on the **Install** button on the right-hand side:

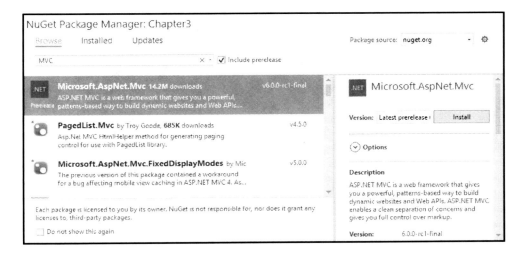

3. Review the changes:

4. Once you click on **Review Changes**, the following dialog box will appear where you need to accept the license terms:

The **NuGet Package Manager** will download and install the ASP.NET Core and will update the `project.json` file and the associated references.

Now, your `project.json` file will have updated dependencies. The second line `Microsoft.AspNet.Mvc` is added:

```
"dependencies": {
  "Microsoft.AspNet.IISPlatformHandler": "1.0.0-rc1-final",
  "Microsoft.AspNet.Mvc": "6.0.0-rc1-final",
  "Microsoft.AspNet.Server.Kestrel": "1.0.0-rc1-final"
},
```

Alternatively, you can also update the `project.json` with the NuGet package along with the version information. The **NuGet Package Manager** will automatically download and install them.

ASP.NET Core is installed in our application. Now, we need to tell our application to use ASP.NET MVC.

This needs a couple of changes to the `Startup.cs` file:

1. Configure the application to add the MVC service. This can be done by adding the following line to the `ConfigureServices` method of the `Startup` class:

   ```
   services.AddMvc();
   ```

2. Configure the routing so that our correct controllers will be picked for the incoming requests based on the URL entered. The following code snippet needs to be updated in the `Configure` method of the `Startup.cs` file:app.UseMvc(routes => {

```
app.UseMvc(routes => {
  routes.MapRoute(
    name: "default",
    template: "{controller=Home}/{action=Index}/{id?}");
});
```

In the preceding statement, we are configuring the routes for our application.

In this chapter and most of the chapters in this book, we will write codes manually or choose an **Empty** template instead of relying on scaffolding templates. For those who are new to the term **scaffolding**, scaffolding is a feature that generates all the necessary boilerplate code for you for the selected item (for example, the Controller) instead of you needing to write everything. Though I agree that scaffolding templates are useful and save time in generating the boilerplate code, they hide many of the details that beginners have to understand. Once you write code manually, you'll know all the intricacies of how each of the components is contributing to the big picture. Once you are strong in the fundamentals, you can use scaffolding templates to save you time in writing the boilerplate code.

Our first Controller

Before creating the Controller, we need to remove the following `app.Run` statement as this will return `Hello World!` for all the incoming requests. As we want incoming requests to be handled by the controllers, we need to remove the following code from the `Configure` method of the `Startup` class:

```
app.Run(async (context) => {
  await context.Response.WriteAsync("Hello World!");
});
```

We have installed the ASP.NET Core in our application. So, we are geared up to creating our first ASP.NET Core controller. Create a folder with the name `Controllers` and add a new Controller by selecting from the context menu as shown in the following screenshot:

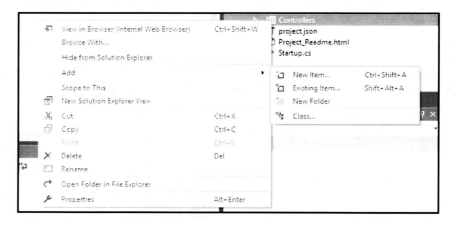

Once you select **Add | New Item**, you will be shown the following list of options. We are going to add an MVC controller class to our project:

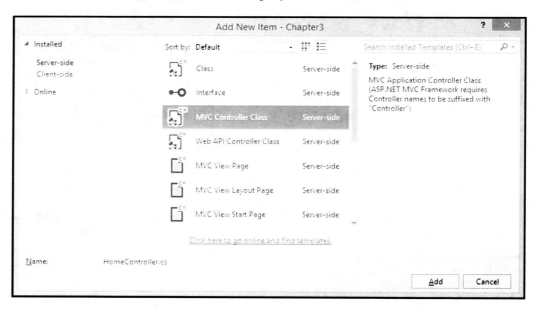

A class will be created with the following content:

```
public class HomeController : Controller {
  // GET: /<controller>/
  public IActionResult Index() {
    return View();
  }
}
```

All controllers, both MVC and Web API controllers, inherit from the `Controller` base class. In earlier versions of ASP.NET MVC, MVC controllers would inherit from the `Controller` class and Web API controllers would inherit from the `APIController` class.

In the preceding `HomeController` class, we have a single action method by `Index` that returns the corresponding View. When you run the application as it is, you'll get a **500 Internal Server Error**. The reason being is that no View has been created for the `Index` action of the `HomeController` and ASP.NET Core tries to search for that View. As the View is not available, it returns a **500 Internal Server Error**.

Instead of creating and returning that View, let us make a simple change to this action method. Let us return a string, `Hello World! I am learning MVC 6!`, and change the return type of `IActionResult`:

```
public string Index() {
  return "Hello World! I am learning MVC 6!";
}
```

Run the application. You'll see the **Hello World! I am learning MVC 6!** in your browser as shown in the following screenshot. Please make sure that you remove the `app.Run` statement in the `Configure` method as mentioned earlier:

Voila! We have changed the ASP.NET Core application to render the custom content instead of the boring *Hello World*. What we have done may seem like a marginal improvement, but we have used controllers and action methods in our ASP.NET Core application, which has brought a lot of structure and flexibility to the web application development.

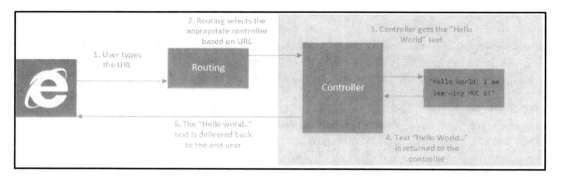

The following is the sequence of steps that occur when we run the application:

1. The application runs on the URL `http://localhost:50140`, where `50140` is the port number selected by IIS Express to run the application on my local system. This number may vary.

2. As we have not passed any parameter, default values for the `Controller` and `action` method will be selected. In our case, `HomeController` will be chosen as the `Controller` and `Index` will be chosen as the `action` method in the `HomeController`. Since `ID` is the optional value and it is not passed, this `ID` parameter is ignored.

3. After the `Controller` and `action` methods are selected by the routing engine, control is passed to the `action` method of the selected controller. In our case, it will be the `Index` action method of the `HomeController`.

4. In the `Index` action method, we are returning a string, `Hello World! I am learning ASP.Net MVC 6!`. This text is returned from the controller, which would then return back to the user.

IActionResult

If you noticed, the default return type in the `action` method of the controller was `IActionResult` and then we changed the return type to the string in order to return the text `Hello World....`

The `IActionResult` is the interface that we can use to return different types of `ActionResult`, ranging from a simple string to complex JSON data, so, we don't need to change the `return` type of the `action` method to return the string.

In the earlier example, I have changed the `return` type to the string to make things simple. Now, let us make a simple change to return the string by keeping the return type (`IActionResult`) as it is:

```
// GET: /<controller>/
public IActionResult Index() {
    return Content("Hello World! I am learning MVC 6!");
}
```

While returning the string, we are using the `virtual` method, called `Content` from the `Controller` class (the base controller from where `HomeController` is inherited from) in the preceding `action` method. The purpose of this `Content()` method is to convert the string to the type `IActionResult`.

Now, run the application. We should be getting the same result.

`IActionResult` is capable of returning different data types:

- `ContentResult`: Can return a text result.
- `EmptyResult`: Returns a `null` result.
- `FileResult`: Returns a binary output to write to the response.
- `HttpStatusCodeResult`: Provides a way to return.
- `JavaScriptResult`: Returns a script that can be executed from the client side.
- `JSonResult`: When you return a serialized JSON object.
- `RedirectResult`: Redirects to another `action` method.
- `RedirectToRouteResult`: Represents a result that performs a redirection by using a specified route values dictionary.

Adding Views

We were returning a simple string from the controller. Although that explains the concept of how the `Controller` and `action` method works, it is not of much practical use.

Let us create a new `action` method by the name, `Index2`:

```
public IActionResult Index2() {
    return View(); // View for this 'Index2' action method
}
```

Now, we have created the `action` method that returns a View. But we still have not added the View for the same. By convention, ASP.NET MVC would try to search for our View in the folder `Views\{ControllerName}\{ActionMethod.cshtml}`. With respect to the preceding example, it will try to search for `Views\Home\Index2.cshtml`. Please note that the name of the `controller` folder-is `Home` , not `HomeController`. Only the prefix is needed as per convention. As this folder structure and file are not available, you'll get a **500 Internal Server Error** when you try to access this action method through the URL `http://localhost:50140/Home/Index2`.

So, let us create a folder structure. Right-click on the solution, select **Add | New Folder** from the context menu, create a folder called `Views`, and then create a subfolder by the name `Home` within the `Views` folder:

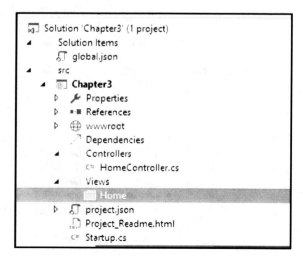

Right click on the `Home` folder, and select **Add** | **New Item** from the context menu. A dialog will appear as shown in the following screenshot. Give the name of the file as `Index2.cshtml`, as our `action` method name is `Index2. cshtml` is the razor view engine (this will be discussed in detail in the *ViewEngines* section of the *Views* chapter) extension used when you are using C#.

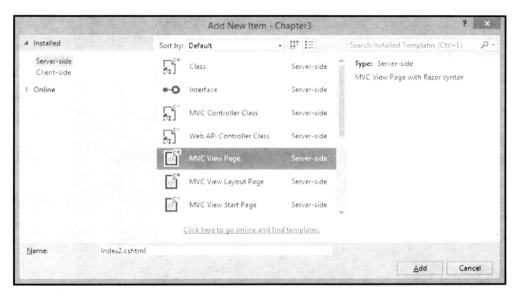

A file by the name `Index2.cshtml` will be created when you click the **Add** button in the preceding screen with the following content:

`@*` is the comment syntax in the razor view engine. You can write any C# code within the `@{ }` block.

Let us add a simple HTML block after the generated code:

```html
<html>
  <body>
    Hello! This is <b>my first View</b>
  </body>
</html>
```

Now, when you run the application, you will get the following output:

The following diagram explains the request flow and how we generate the response through the View:

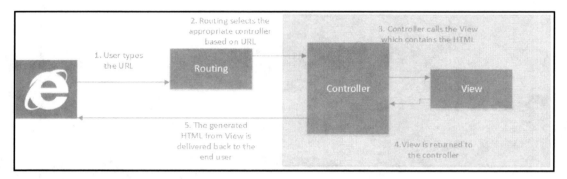

Adding Models

Models represent your business domain classes. Now, we are going to learn about how to use the Models in our controller. Create a `Models` folder and add a simple `Employee` class. This is a just a plain old C# class:

```
public class Employee {
  public int EmployeeId { get; set; }
  public string Name { get; set; }
  public string Designation { get; set; }
}
```

Create a new `action` method, `Employee`, in our `HomeController`, and create an object of the `Employee` Model with some values, and pass the Model to the View. Our idea is to use the Model employee values in the View to present them to the user:

```
using Chapter3.Models;
public IActionResult Employee() {
  //Sample Model - Usually this comes from database
 Employee emp1 = new Employee {
    EmployeeId = 1,
    Name = "Jon Skeet",
    Designation = " Software Architect"
  };
  return View(emp1);
}
```

Now, we need to add the respective View for this `action` method. Add a new Razor view file in the `View\Home folder`.

Add the following code snippet. Whatever comes after the @ symbol is considered as Razor code. In the following code, we are trying to access the properties of the `Model` object that is passed to our view. In our case, `Model` represents the `employee` object that we have constructed in our `action` method. You can access the object from View using the Model keyword:

```
<html>
  <body>
 Employee Name : @Model.Name <br/>
    Employee Designation: @Model.Designation <br/>
  </body>
</html>
```

When you run the application and type the URL
`http://localhost:50140/Home/Employee`, you'll see the following output:

Passing data from Controller to View

We have just discussed how to pass the data from the Controller to the View using the `Model` object. While calling the View, we are passing the model data as a parameter. But there are times when you want to pass some temporary data to the View from the Controller. This temporary data may not deserve a `model` class. In such scenarios, we can use either `ViewBag` or `ViewData`.

`ViewData` is the dictionary and `ViewBag` is the dynamic representation of the same value.

Let us add the company name and company location property using `ViewBag` and `ViewData` as shown in the following code snippet:

```
public IActionResult Employee() {
  //Sample Model - Usually this comes from database
  Employee emp1 = new Employee {
    EmployeeId = 1,
    Name = "Jon Skeet",
    Designation = " Software Architect"
  };

  ViewBag.Company = "Google Inc";
  ViewData["CompanyLocation"] = "United States";

  return View(emp1);
}
```

Make the respective changes in the View file as well so that we can display the `Company name` and `Company location` values:

```
<html>
  <body>
    Employee Name : @Model.Name <br/>
    Employee Designation: @Model.Designation <br/>
    Company : @ViewBag.Company <br/>
    Company Location: @ViewData["CompanyLocation"] <br />
  </body>
</html>
```

Run the application after making the preceding changes:

`ViewBag` and `ViewData` represent the same collection, even though the entries in the collection are accessed through different methods. `ViewBag` values are dynamic values and are executed at run-time, whereas the `ViewData` is accessed through the dictionary.

To test this, let us make a simple change to our `view` file:

```
Employee Name : @Model.Name <br/>
Employee Designation: @Model.Designation <br/>
Company : @ViewData["Company"] <br />
Company Location : @ViewBag.CompanyLocation <br />
```

Even though I have stored the `Company` value using `ViewBag` in the `Controller`, I am accessing the same using `ViewData`. The same is the case for the `Company Location` value, we have stored the value using `ViewData` in the Controller, but we are accessing the value using `ViewBag`.

When you run the application after making the preceding changes, you'll see the same result as you have seen before.

Filters

Filters in ASP.NET MVC enable you to run code before or after a particular stage in the execution pipeline. They can be configured globally per-controller or per-action.

There are different kinds of filters, and each filter is executed at a different stage in the pipeline. For example, action filters are executed when the `action` method is executed.

Let us use a simple example to see how an action filter (a type of filter) works.

I have created a simple controller, `DateController`, where I am just displaying the time. In this `action` method, I am using a predefined action filter by the name of `ResponseCache`, that caches the response for the duration specified in seconds. In the following code snippet, we have mentioned the duration as 600 seconds. So, the response will be cached for 10 minutes.

```
public class DateController : Controller {
  [ResponseCache(Duration = 600)]
  public IActionResult Index() {
    return Content(DateTime.Now.ToShortTimeString());
  }
}
```

When I run it for the first time, it displays the time as expected. But when you refresh the browser (which indirectly fires the request again), the time is not updated as the response is cached already by the application. In the following screenshot, even though the time is 7:43, the application is still showing as 7:40:

The following are the predefined types of filters available in ASP.NET Core.

Authorization filters

These are used for authorization and are mainly intended to determine whether the current user is authorized for the request being made.

Resource filters

These are the filters that handle the request after authorization and are the last one to handle the request before it leaves the filter pipeline. They are used to implement caching or by passing the filter pipeline.

Action filters

These wrap calls to individual `action` method calls and can manipulate the arguments passed in the action as well as the action result returned from it.

Exception filters

These are used to manage the unhandled exceptions in ASP.NET MVC.

Result filters

This wrap the individual action results and they only run when the `action` method is executed successfully.

Summary

In this chapter, we have built our first ASP.NET 5 application from scratch and we have installed ASP.NET Core in our ASP.NET 5 application. We have learned how the controller fits into the overall ASP.NET MVC application and learned how to build your first controller with the `action` methods. We also learned about how to use Model and View in our Controller. We have also discussed different ways to pass the data from the Controller to the View using `ViewBag` and `ViewData`. We have also learned about filters in ASP.NET MVC and how to make use of predefined filters in ASP.NET Core.

4

Views

Views are the actual output of the application that is delivered to the user. It is what they actually see when they access your application from the screen. All the components, be it menus, input elements, dialog boxes, and everything the user sees comes from your Views only. If you do not provide good user experience when accessing your application, users will not care how great your application is. So, Views play a critical role when building an ASP.NET MVC application.

In this chapter, we'll cover the following topics:

- The purpose of View Engine and Razor View Engine
- Programming in Razor View Engine and different programming constructs
- Layout in ASP.NET Core and its features
- HTML Helpers
- Partial Views
- Tag Helpers

The View engine and the Razor View engine

As discussed in `Chapter 1`, *Introduction to ASP.NET Core*, a browser can only understand HTML, CSS, and JavaScript. The purpose of the View engine is to generate the HTML code from your View and send it to the browser so that it can understand the content. Primarily, there are two different types of View engines—Razor View engine and Webform View engine. Although these two View engines come out of the box with ASP.NET MVC, you can use any custom View engine.

Razor View engine

The Razor View engine is the default and recommended View engine in ASP.NET Core, and going forward, this may be the only View engine coming out of the box when you install ASP.NET MVC.

You can mix a C# code and HTML code in your Razor View and the Razor View engine is intelligent enough to distinguish between these two and generate the expected output. In some scenarios, we may have to give additional information to Razor View to produce the appropriate results. Razor code blocks start with the @ symbol and do not require a closing @.

Programming in Razor View engine

Programming in Razor View engine is just like you program in C#. The difference is that, in Razor View engine, your C# code will get mixed with HTML to produce the desired HTML output.

Variables in Razor View

You can declare a variable inside the razor block and use that variable using the @ symbol.

 For all the examples in this chapter, we will only present the code samples of the view.

Let's discuss this with an example.

1. Create a `Controllers` folder and a Controller called `HomeController`.
2. Create a folder called `Views`, a subfolder called `Home`, and a View file called `Index.cshtml` by right-clicking the context menu and selecting **Add** | **New Item** and then **MVC Razor View** from the list.

The `HomeController.cs` file will have following code:

```
public class HomeController : Controller
{
  // GET: /<controller>/
  public IActionResult Index()
  {
    return View();
```

```
    }
  }
```

Next is the updated Razor View where we will declare a variable and use it. The first five lines and the last two lines are simple HTML elements.

We will concentrate on the lines that are bold. Then, we will create a Razor block using @ { … } and declaring a variable inside it. The Razor block ends with the closing curly bracket. The snippet Value: is considered as simple HTML text. As we would like to use the razor variable value, we will use @i to instruct the Razor View engine that i is not a normal HTML text; and it is a Razor construct and is to be treated accordingly. The complete HTML code is as follows:

```
<html>
  <head>
    <title> Views demo</title>
  </head>
  <body>
    @{
        int i = 5;
    }
    Value: @i
  </body>
</html>
```

When you run the application, you'll see the following output:

Please note that when you access the razor variable, you will need to use the @ symbol. Without this, Razor View engine sees the i as text and not as an expression.

The following screenshot is the result you will get when you access the variable without @ symbol:

The for loop

You can use most of the programming constructs available in C# in Razor View. The following piece of code is the `for` loop construct where we loop through five times and print the variable name:

```
@{
    for (int i = 0; i < 5; i++)
    {
      <li>@(i+1)</li>
    }
}
```

The following are a few points to be noted:

- As the for loop is a razor code, we should enclose the loop with the @ symbol to indicate that the code that follows is a Razor code and not normal HTML.
- Whenever we use an HTML element or tag, Razor View engine falls back to HTML mode. If you want to use any Razor expression within the HTML tags, you will want to include the @ symbol again to tell the Razor View engine that whatever follows is a Razor code and not an HTML element. This is the reason we use the @ symbol again in the preceding expression, even within the parent root-level razor code.

The complete code for the View is as follows:

```
<html>
  <head>
    <title> Views demo</title>
  </head>
  <body>
    <ul>
    @{
        for (int i = 0; i < 5; i++)
        {
          <li>@(i+1)</li>
        }
```

```
    }
   </ul>
  </body>
</html>
```

The while loop

The following piece of code is the `while` loop implementation for the same loop. Please note that the emboldened expressions increment the variable i. We will not use the @ symbol as it is not within the HTML element:

```
@{
    int i = 0;
    while(i<5)
    {
      <li>@(i + 1)</li>
      i++;
    }
  }
```

The foreach loop

The `foreach` loop in Razor View is the same as the `foreach` loop in C#. In the following code, we will initialize a list of integers, iterate through the list and print it as a list item:

```
<ul>
  @{
    List<int> integers = new List<int>
    {
      1,2,3,4,5
    };
    foreach (int i in integers)
    {
      <li>@i</li>
    }
  }
</ul>
```

The if condition

In the following code, we will check if the value of the variable is less than 10. If it is less than 10, we will print i is less than 10, otherwise, we will say i is greater than 10. You may wonder why we have to include the text tag and what its purpose is. As we are inside the Razor View code block, the text i is less than 10 will be considered as Razor expression, but it is not.

This `text` tag is to instruct the Razor View engine that whatever follows the `text` tag is to be considered as a text and not as a Razor expression:

```
@{
    int i = 5;
    if (i < 10)
    {
      <text>i is less than 10</text>
    }
    else
    {
      <text>i is greater than 10</text>
    }
}
```

Layout

In all the previous examples we discussed, we have done the complete View coding in a single file. This will result in a lack of flexibility and reduced reusability.

Consider the following web page structure where the **Top Section** contains the company logo or banner and the **Side Section** contains the links to various sections of the site. The **Content Section** changes for every page.

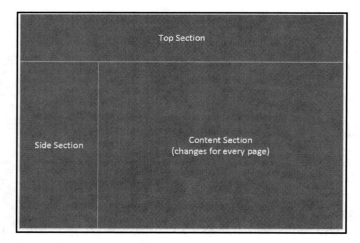

If we code the complete content in a single view, we may have to duplicate the **Top Section** and **Side Section** in every page. If we want to change anything in the **Side Section**, we will have to change all the files. This clearly shows that a single View file is not the best solution.

The layout comes to the rescue in this scenario. The layout defines the site structure that can be reused across all the web pages. The layout does not even need to have something like the top section or side section; it can contain even a simple HTML structure where you can have common content and the body content will be rendered from individual view.

Let's build our first layout. In order to use the layout, you will need to have the following three things:

1. Inform the name of the layout file—this information should be made available in _ViewStart.cshtml. By convention, the names of all the shared files will start with an underscore and this file is located directly under the Views folder.
2. Create the Layout file—by convention, the name of the file is _Layout.cshtml and it will be located in the Shared folder. All the shared content, such as partial views, will also be available here. Partial Views will be discussed later in this chapter.
3. Create the content View file—this View file is almost same as the earlier View files that we created so far with only one difference; only page-specific content will be available in this file, and this means that you'll not have any html, head, or title tags here.

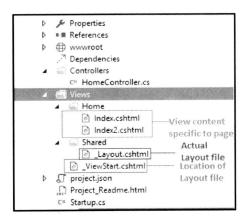

After the creation of _ViewStart.cshtml, _Layout.cshtml, and page-specific View files, the folder structure will be like the preceding snapshot.

Creating _ViewStart.cshtml

Right-click on the **Views** folder and select **Add New Item** from the **Context** menu. Then, select **MVC View Start Page** from the **Add New Item** dialog box as shown in the following screenshot:

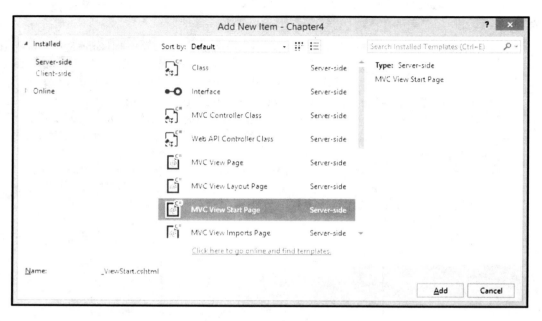

When you click the **Add** button, it will create a file with the following content:

```
@{
    Layout = "_Layout";
}
```

Creating _Layout.cshtml

Create a folder called **Shared** within the **Views** folder. Then, right-click on the **Shared** folder and select **Add New Item** from the **Context** menu as shown in the following screenshot:

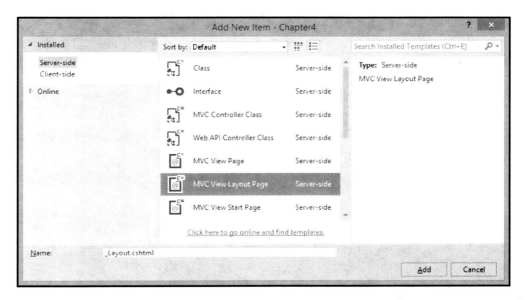

When you click the **Add** button, it will create **_Layout.cshtml** with the following content:

```
<!DOCTYPE html>
<html>
<head>
<meta name="viewport" content="width=device-width" />
<title>@ViewBag.Title</title>
</head>
<body>
<div>
@RenderBody()
</div>
</body>
</html>
```

The preceding layout file is a simple HTML content with a couple of Razor expressions. @ViewBag. The title is used to display the title information passed from the Controller and @RenderBody is the Razor expression that calls the page specific View and merges that content over there.

Adding a page-specific View

Before adding the View, we will need to add an action method in our HomeController file from which we will be calling our page-specific view.

Let's add an action method named `Index2` as follows:

```
public IActionResult Index2()
{
  ViewBag.Title = "This is Index2";
  return View();
}
```

The `ViewBag` is used to pass information from the Controller to the View. Here, we are passing the `Title` information from the action method to the View.

Now, right-click on the `Views` folder, select **Add** | **New Item**, select **MVC View Page**, and save the file as `Index2.cshtml`.

In the generated view, I have added simple `Hello` text. This text will be rendered in the body of the layout page. The complete code of the View file is as follows:

```
@*
For more information on enabling MVC for empty projects, visit
http://go.microsoft.com/fwlink/?LinkID=397860
*@
@{
  ...
}
Hello. This text will be rendered in body of the layout page
```

Everything is set now. Run the application and type the URL `http://localhost:50132/Home/Index2` in the browser. Please note that the port number after the local host may vary when you run the application from your PC.

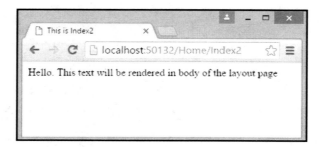

As expected, you'll see the text seen in the preceding picture. However, our point is not about the text. It's about the structure of the generated HTML content.

View the source by pressing *Ctrl + U* (on the Chrome browser in Windows). You'll see the following HTML content:

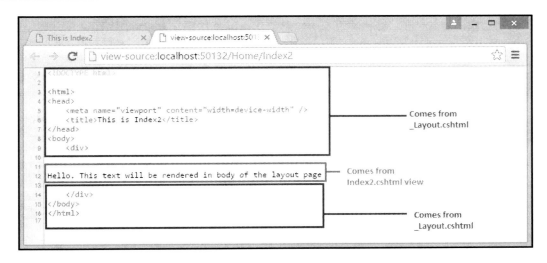

The top content (the `html`, `head`, `body`, and `div` opening tags) and bottom content (the `html`, `head`, `body`, and `div` closing tags) come from the layout file and the text comes from the View specific to the page.

Generating HTML

As discussed in `Chapter 1`, *Introduction to ASP.NET Core*, browsers can understand only HTML, CSS, and JavaScript, irrespective of the technology that you use to build the web application. This holds true when building the application in ASP.NET MVC as well.

Most applications get the user input, process the input, and then store the required information in the database to retrieve them later. In the context of web applications, Form HTML elements are used to get the user input.

The following are a couple of ways to generate HTML elements in ASP.NET Core:

- HTML Helpers
- Tag Helpers

HTML Helpers are server-side methods that aid in generating HTML elements, which can be understood by the browsers. HTML helpers were the primary method of generating the HTML elements up till ASP.NET MVC 5.

Tag Helpers, introduced in ASP.NET Core, also produce HTML elements. Tag helpers, which we will discuss in a later section of this chapter, will look just like HTML elements where you add attributes to identify them as Tag Helpers. The advantage of using Tag helpers over HTML helpers is that the user interfaces designers/engineers do not need to worry about Razor code. They just code with HTML elements and additional attributes.

Before discussing HTML helpers and Tag helpers, let's take a step back and talk about why we need them in the first place.

Let's consider a simple form, as shown in the following picture, where we would like to get the user's name and their age. If the user enters her age, we will display You are eligible to vote!. If not, we will display You are not eligible to vote now:

The following is the HTML code to show the preceding simple form:

```html
<form>
  <table>
    <tr>
      <td>
        <label for="txtName">Name</label>
      </td>
      <td>
        <input type="text" id="txtName" />
      </td>
    </tr>
    <tr>
      <td>
        <label for="txtAge">Age</label>
      </td>
      <td>
        <input type="text" id="txtAge" />
      </td>
    </tr>
    <tr>
      <td colspan="2">
        <input type="submit"  />
      </td>
    </tr>
  </table>
</form>
```

This method of coding HTML elements directly is time-consuming and error-prone. For example, in the preceding form, the label and input HTML elements refer to the same element (txtName in the first group and txtAge in the second group). If we hand-code the HTML element, there is a possibility of a typo error in building the HTML element.

HTML Helpers

HTML helpers are server-side methods that generate HTML for you. We can generate the same form using HTML helpers as follows (HTML.BeginForm, @Html.Label, and @Html.TextBox generate the HTML form element, label, and textbox elements, respectively):

```
@using (Html.BeginForm())
  {
    <table>
      <tr>
        <td>@Html.Label("Name")</td>
        <td>@Html.TextBox("txtName")</td>
      </tr>
      <tr>
        <td>@Html.Label("Age")</td>
        <td>@Html.TextBox("txtAge")</td>
      </tr>
      <tr>
        <td colspan="2"><input type="submit" value="Submit" /></td>
      </tr>
    </table>
  }
```

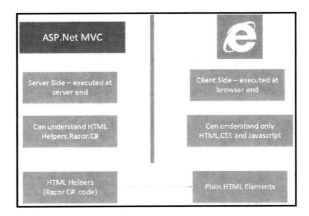

You might wonder why we need to use HTML helpers when we can write the HTML code manually. Things will get more complex when we pass the model from the Controller to the view. Using HTML helpers, we can directly build `form` elements from `Models` files so that they will pick the names from the `Models` that you are using.

For example, let's create a folder called `Models` and a class called `Person`. This class will act as a model as shown in the following screenshot:

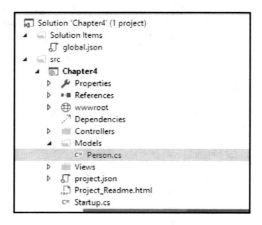

The `Person` class is just a POCO (Plain Old C# Object) class and will act as a model. The complete code for this class is as follows:

```
public class Person
{
  public int PersonId { get; set; }
  public string Name { get; set; }
  public int Age { get; set; }
}
```

Let's create a new action method called `ValidateAge`. In this method, we will create an empty `Person` class and pass the Model to the View. We will also create a dynamic property called `Title` in `ViewBag` so that we can display this value in View:

```
[HttpGet]
public IActionResult ValidateAge()
{
  ViewBag.Title = "Validate Age for voting";
  Person person1 = new Person();
  return View(person1);
}
```

In the view, create the form using the following HTML Helpers:

```
@model Chapter4.Models.Person
@using (Html.BeginForm("ValidateAge", "Home", FormMethod.Post))
 {
    <table>
      <tr>
        <td>@Html.LabelFor(Model => Model.Name) </td>
        <td>@Html.TextBoxFor(Model => Model.Name) </td>
      </tr>
      <tr>
        <td>@Html.LabelFor(Model => Model.Age)</td>
        <td>@Html.TextBoxFor(Model => Model.Age)</td>
      </tr>
      <tr>
        <td colspan="2"><input type="submit" value="Submit" /></td>
      </tr>
    </table>
 }
```

In the first line, we are telling the View that we are passing the Model of type Person class. This enables you to use the strong type of Model, that is, when you type Model and a dot, **IntelliSense** provides you with all the properties of the Person class

In the second line, we are using the overloaded BeginForm HTML helpers which accept three parameters—the action method name, the Controller name, and the Form method.

Simply, when the user submits the form, the information should be passed to the mentioned action of the Controller.

In the LabelFor and TextBox For HTML helpers, we are just passing Model properties (name and age); it automatically queries and gets the Model properties and builds the respective HTML elements. This is one of the primary advantages of using HTML helpers. Without using the HTML helpers, this process might become complex.

Now, let's write the respective POST action method in the same way. In the following POST action method, based on the age entered in the form, we set the dynamic property as Message.

```
[HttpPost]
public IActionResult ValidateAge(Person person1)
{
  if(person1.Age>=18)
  {
    ViewBag.Message = "You are eligible to Vote!";
  }
```

```
  else
  {
    ViewBag.Message = "Sorry.You are not old enough to vote!";
  }
  return View();
}
```

It is to be noted that both the GET and POST action method refer to the same View —ValidateAge.cshtml. Add the following content to the View just above the form element:

```
@if(ViewBag.Message!=null)
  {
    <b>@ViewBag.Message</b>
  }
```

Once the user submits the form, the POST action method sets the dynamic Message property in ViewBag. However, the value of this property will be null when the View is rendered as part of the GET request. If the value is not null, insert the message at the top of the page.

When you run the application, you'll get the following output:

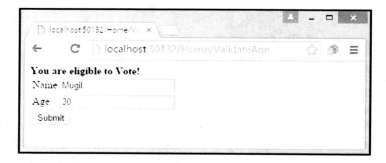

Partial View

Partial Views are just Views that can be reused across your application. Partial Views can be thought of as pluggable reusable blocks that you can call from anywhere and have the content of the partial view displayed.

Consider the following structure of a web page—it's the same layout page that we used earlier, but with a couple of changes. The **Latest News** block is added to the **Side Section** and the **Login** block is added to the **Top Section**. These blocks are not restricted to the **Top Section** or **Side Section** and can be used anywhere in your application, including your **Content Section** as shown in the following figure:

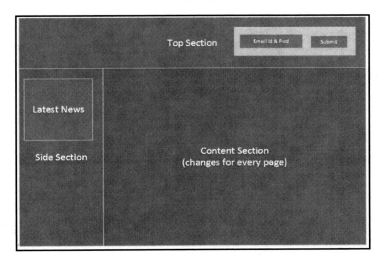

These Partial Views are not restricted to static content and can contain `form` elements. In the preceding screenshot, the **Latest News** Partial View contains the text content and the login Partial View contains `form` elements to get the e-mail ID and password.

Location of Partial Views—Framework does not restrict the location of the Partial View. However, by convention, if your Partial View will be used only by your Controller, you can create that Partial View in the Controller-specific Views folder. For example, if your Partial View will only be used in `HomeController` file, you can create that Partial View in the `Views\Home` folder.

Let's take look at how to create a Partial View and use it.

As discussed earlier, a Partial View is just like a normal View. So, we will create a Partial View in the same way we create normal View.

Right-click on the `Shared` folder and select **Add | New Item**. By convention, like all shared content, the name of the Partial View will also start with "_"(underscore), as shown in the following screenshot:

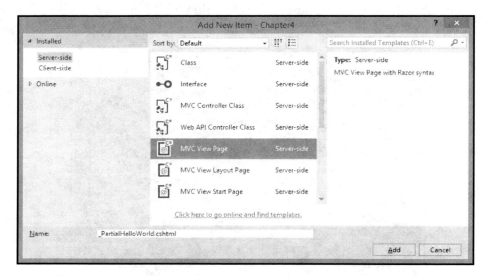

We are creating this Partial View based on the assumption that it can be used from anywhere in the application.

In the generated Partial View, I have added the following simple static content—a text and a simple table:

```html
<b>This content and below table is coming from partial view</b>
<table border="1">
  <tr>
    <th>Employee No</th>
    <th>Employee Name</th>
  </tr>
  <tr>
    <td>10012</td>
    <td>Jon Skeet</td>
  </tr>
  <tr>
    <td>10013</td>
    <td>Scott Guthrie</td>
  </tr>
</table>
```

Calling the Partial View

A Partial View can be called using the @Html.Partial HTML helper.

In our case, we will be calling the Partial View from Index2.cshtml file. The parameter that you pass will be the name of the partial file. It will search for the Partial View by that name and render that complete content as part of the Index2.cshtml file.

The content of Index2.html file will now be as follows:

```
Hello. This text will be rendered in body of the layout page<br/> <br/>
<br/>

@Html.Partial("_PartialHelloWorld")
```

Now, run the application and access the URL http://localhost:50132/Home/Index2. You'll see the following output:

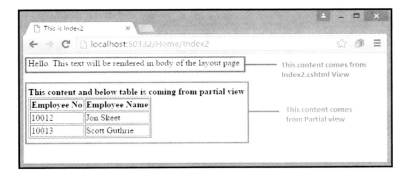

View components

View components are a new feature introduced in ASP.NET Core, they are almost similar to Partial Views but is more powerful. When you use Partial Views, you have dependency over the Controller. However, when you use the ViewComponent attribute, you do not have to depend on the Controller, so we will establish separation of concerns and have better testability. Even though the existing Partial View HTML helper is still supported, it is preferable to use the View component whenever you want to show a reusable piece of information when you are using .NET Core.

Creating a View component

You can create a `ViewComponent` using any of the following:

- Create a class by deriving from the `ViewComponent` attribute
- Decorate a class with the `[ViewComponent]` attribute or derive it from the class that has the `[ViewComponent]` attribute
- You can use the convention by creating a class that ends with a suffix `ViewComponent` attribute

Whatever option you choose, this `ViewComponent` should be public, non-nested, and non-abstract classes.

Like Controllers, you can use the Dependency Injection (via a constructor) in the `ViewComponent` attribute as well. As the `ViewComponent` attribute is separate from the Controller lifecycle, you may not be able to use the action filters in `ViewComponents`.

There is a method called `Invoke` (or `InvokeAync`, the asynchronous equivalent of `Invoke`), that will return the `IComponentViewResult` interface. This method is similar to the action method of the Controller that will return the View.

Let's get our hands dirty by creating a `ViewComponent` attribute.

Create a new folder called `ViewComponents` in your project and a new class called `SimpleViewComponent`, as shown in the following screenshot:

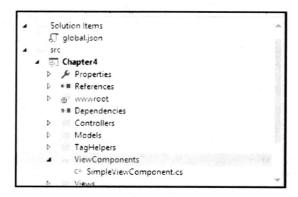

The `SimpleViewComponent` file that we created will look like the following:

```
using System;
using System.Collections.Generic;
using System.Linq;
```

```
using System.Threading.Tasks;
using Microsoft.AspNet.Mvc;

namespace Chapter4.ViewComponents
{
  public class SimpleViewComponent :ViewComponent
  {
    public IViewComponentResult Invoke()
    {
      var data = GetSampleData();
      return View(data);
    }
    /// <summary>
    /// This is a simple private method to return some dummy data
    /// </summary>
    /// <returns></returns>

    private List<string> GetSampleData()
    {
      List<string> data = new List<string>();
      data.Add("One");
      data.Add("Two");
      data.Add("Three");
      return data;
    }
  }
}
```

We just have a couple of methods, one to populate the data and the other is the `Invoke` method where we will render the View.

Once you have created the `ViewComponent` attribute, you will need to include the `ViewComponent` namespace in the `Views\_ViewImports.cshtml` file so that the `ViewComponents` attributes can be available for all the Views. The highlighted code snippet in the following is added to the View:

```
@using Chapter4
@using Chapter4.Models
@using Chapter4.ViewComponents
@addTagHelper "*, Microsoft.AspNet.Mvc.TagHelpers"
```

We have created the `ViewComponent` and made them available to all of the Views. A simple action method in the `HomeController` file just returns the View:

```
public ActionResult Sample()
{
return View();
```

```
}
```

In the associated View, we can just invoke the component as shown in the following code snippet:

```
<p>
  This is a sample web page <br/>
  <div>
    @Component.Invoke("Simple")
  </div>
</p>
```

When you invoke the component, it will search in the following two folders:

- The `Views\<controller_name>\Components\<view component name>\<view name>` folder
- The `Views\Shared\Components\<view_component_name>/<view_name>` folder

The default View name of the View component is `Default`, which makes your file name for the View `Default.cshtml`. So, we will need to create the `Default.cshtml` file in `Views\Shared\Simple\Default.cshtml` folder, as shown in the following screenshot:

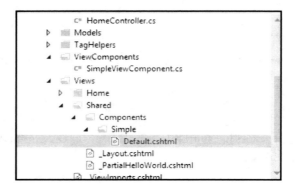

In the the View (`Default.cshtml` file) of the `ViewComponent` file, we are just iterating the items in the model and displaying them as an unordered list item, as shown in the following code:

```
@model IEnumerable<string>

<h3> Sample list</h3>
<ul>
  @foreach(var item in Model)
```

```
  {
     <li>@item</li>
  }
</ul>
```

When you run the application and access the URL
(`http://localhost:50132/Home/Sample`), you should see the following output:

The first line, **This is a sample web page**, comes from the parent View file
(`sample.cshtml`) whereas the subsequent list comes from `ViewComponent` attribute.

The `ViewComponent` attributes are usually referred in the Views. However, if you want to
call the `ViewComponent` directly from your Controller, you can do so.

I have called the `Sample` action method to call the Simple `ViewComponent` directly instead
of calling it through some other View as follows:

```
public ActionResult Sample()
{
   return ViewComponent("Simple");
   //return View();
}
```

Thus, these `ViewComponents` have far more flexibility and features, such as Dependency Injection, when compared to old HTML Partial Views. This ensures `ViewComponents` are separately tested.

Tag Helpers

Tag Helpers are a new feature in ASP.NET Core; they help generate the HTML elements. In HTML helpers, we will write a C#/Razor code to generate the HTML. The disadvantage associated with this approach is that many frontend engineers will not know C#/Razor code. They work on plain HTML, CSS, and JavaScript. Tag Helpers look just like HTML code but have all the features of server-side rendering. You can even build your custom Tag Helper for your needs.

Let's take a look at how to use a Tag Helper. In order to use the Tag helper, you will need to install the `Microsoft.AspNet.Mvc.TagHelpers` NuGet package.

Open the **Package Manager Console** window by selecting **View | Other Windows | Package Manager Console**, as shown in the following screenshot:

You can install `TagHelpers` methods by entering the following command in the **Package Manager Console** window, the following command:

```
Install-Package Microsoft.AspNet.Mvc.TagHelpers -Pre
```

The following response will appear when you've entered the command:

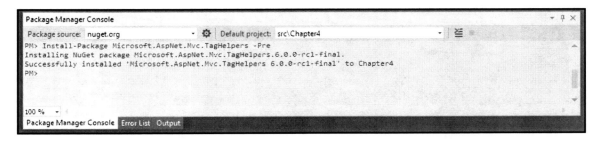

Once the `TagHelpers` package is installed, we will need to call `ViewImports` file, where we will add the `TagHelpers` directive so that Tag Helpers are available to our Views.

Right-click on the `Views` folder and select the **Add New Item** option from the **Context** menu; you'll see the following screen:

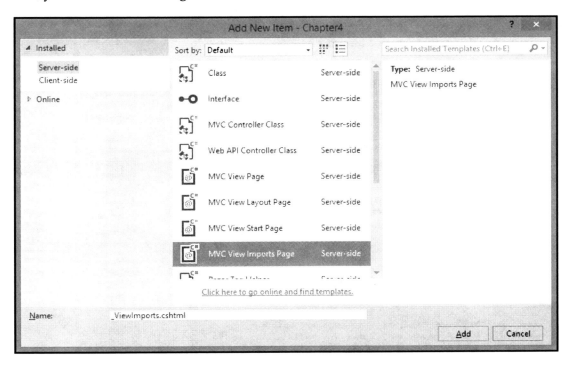

Add the following content to the `_ViewImports.cs` file. The first couple of lines tells ASP.NET MVC to include the necessary namespaces. The last line tells ASP.NET MVC to include all the `TagHelpers` available in `Microsoft.AspNet.Mvc.TagHelpers`. The first parameter indicates the name of TagHelper. We have used *, which means that we may want to use all the Tag Helpers. The second parameter indicates the assembly where the `TagHelpers` will be available:

```
@using Chapter4
@using Chapter4.Models
@addTagHelper "*, Microsoft.AspNet.Mvc.TagHelpers"
```

As we are creating the `_ViewImports.cshtml` file directly under the `Views` folder, as shown in the following screenshot, the Tag Helpers will be available for all the Views:

Had we included the `_ViewImports.cshtml` file under the `Home` folder, the Tag Helpers would be available only for the Views under the `Home` folder.

Let's add a simple action method called `Index3` in the `HomeController` file, and in the associated View, we will use Tag Helpers as shown in the following code:

```
public IActionResult Index3()
{
  ViewBag.Title = "This is Index3";
  Person person = new Person();
  return View(person);
}
```

Add the corresponding View (`Index3.cshtml` file) for the `Index3` action method with the following code:

```
@model Chapter4.Models.Person
<form asp-controller="Home" asp-action="Index3">
  <table>
    <tr>
      <td><labelasp-for="Name"></label></td>
      <td><input asp-for="Name" /></td>
    </tr>
    <tr>
      <td><labelasp-for="Age"></label></td>
      <td><inputasp-for="Age" /></td>
```

```
      </tr>
      <tr>
        <td colspan="2"><input type="submit" value="Submit" /></td>
      </tr>
    </table>
  </form>
```

The following are a few things that you need to note in the preceding code, for the use of Tag Helpers:

- All the form elements look just like standard HTML elements with just a few changes in the attributes. This makes frontend developers work independently, without learning HTML/Razor code and thus more easily achieving the separation which concerns.
- The first line of the preceding view indicates the type of model data passed to the view from the Controller.
- The Form element has a couple of attributes named `asp-controller` and `asp-action` which represent Controller names and action method names respectively.
- The Label and input tag helpers are just like HTML elements, with just an additional `asp-for` attribute. The values for these attributes represent the model properties. You can take advantage of IntelliSense when entering the values for these attributes.

Creating custom Tag Helpers

ASP.NET Core provides many built-in Tag Helpers to help you create the necessary HTML elements for many scenarios. However, this process is not comprehensive and is exhaustive. Sometimes, you may want to make some changes in the generated HTML element, or you may want to create an HTML element with new properties or a new HTML element altogether. You are not restricted to using only the existing Tag Helpers in the ASP.NET Core application. You can create your own Tag Helper if the existing Tag Helpers do not suit your needs. Let's create a simple Tag Helper to create an e-mail link:

```
<a href="mailto:mugil@dotnetodyssey.com">
```

There are a couple of ways to create Tag Helpers to implement the `ITagHelper` interface or inherit the `TagHelper` class. The `TagHelper` class has a `Process` method that you can override to write your custom Tag Helpers. The `TagHelper` class also has the `TagHelperOutput` parameter, which you can use to write and generate the desired output HTML. So, it is preferable to create Tag Helpers by inheriting from the `TagHelper` class.

Our objective is to write a custom e-mail Tag Helper so that when someone uses that Tag Helper, which is `<email mailTo="mugil@greatestretailstore.com"></email>`, it should be converted to the following line of code:

```
<a href="mailto:mugil@greatestretailstore.com">Drop us a mail</a>
```

The following are the steps that need to be performed to create the custom Tag Helper in the ASP.NET Core application.

Create a folder called `TagHelper` and add a new item named the `EmailTagHelper.cs` file. By convention, all Tag Helpers class should end with `TagHelper`, even though we can override this convention.

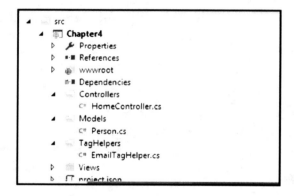

Once you have created the file, you will need to override the `Process` method to generate the desired HTML output:

```
using System;
using System.Collections.Generic;
using System.Linq;
using System.Threading.Tasks;
using Microsoft.AspNet.Razor.TagHelpers;

namespace Chapter4.TagHelpers
{
    public class EmailTagHelper : TagHelper
```

```
    {
        public override void Process(TagHelperContext context, TagHelperOutput
    output)
        {
            string emailTo= context.AllAttributes["mailTo"].Value.ToString();
            output.TagName = "a";
            output.Attributes["href"] = "mailto:" + emailTo;
            output.Content.SetContent("Drop us a mail");
        }
    }
}
```

The parameters used in the preceding code are explained as follows:

- The `context` parameter will give you all the information that you supply at Tag Helper. For example, in the `<emailmailTo="mugil@greatestretailstore.com"></email>` Tag Helper, you can get the `mailTo` attribute and its associated value from the `context` parameter. In the first line of the preceding `Process` method, we will get the `mailTo` attribute value and use that value to create an attribute in the generated HTML (anchor tag).
- The `output` parameter is of type `TagHelperOutput`, which is used to generate the desired HTML output.
- The `output.Content.SetContent` parameter will set the text that is to be displayed for the anchor tag.

We have created the e-mail Tag Helper. Now, we have to make it available to our Views so that we can make use of that Tag Helper in our Views. Edit `Views\_ViewImports.cshtml` to include the namespace of the `TagHelpers` and add the associated `TagHelpers`. In the following _ViewImports.cshtml file, we have added the content highlighted in bold:

```
@using Chapter4
@using Chapter4.Models
@using Chapter4.TagHelpers
@addTagHelper "*, Microsoft.AspNet.Mvc.TagHelpers"
@addTagHelper "*, Chapter4"
```

The "*" symbol in the following line tells the view engine to include all the TagHelpers in the `Chapter4` namespace:

```
@addTagHelper "*, Chapter4"
```

You can only specific `TagHelpers`, For example, the following line will include only the `EmailTagHelper` so it is available for our Views:

```
@addTagHelper "Chapter4.TagHelpers.EmailTagHelper, Chapter4"
```

Let's create a simple action method in our Home Controller. In the view of the associated action method, we will use the e-mail Tag Helper:

```
public IActionResult AboutUs()
{
  return View();
}
```

The following is the view of the preceding `AboutUs` action method:

```
<h3>About Us</h3>
We are one of the biggest electronics retail store serving millions of
people across the nation. blah.blah. blah <br/>

If you want to hear great offers from us
<email mailTo="mugil@greatestretailstore.com"></email>
```

When you run the application and access the `http://localhost:50132/Home/AboutUs` URL, you will see the following output:

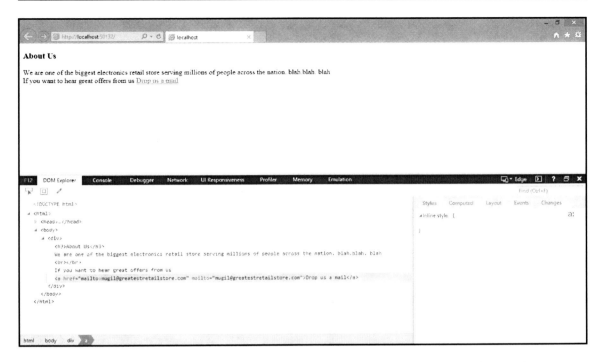

Here, we created an anchor tag with the `mailto` attribute and the email value as the `href` attribute value.

I have opened the **Developer Tools** window (Press *F12* to do this and select the **DOM Explorer** tab) to see the generated HTML.

Summary

In this chapter, you learned what a View engine is and how to build a View using the Razor view engine. We also discussed different programming constructs that you can make use of in Razor to produce the desired HTML output. Then, you learned about Layout and how to provide a consistent site structure across all of the pages in your ASP.NET MVC application. Later, we discussed how to promote re-usability using Partial Views with an example. Finally, you learned how to use Tag Helpers to produce clean HTML.

5

Models

Data is the heart of every application. A user enters data into the application, edits the entered data, and searches the data. We can even say that an application that we build is just an interface for the operations that we perform on the application data. So, it is absolutely necessary for any framework to provide a mechanism to handle data operations easier and more manageable. Models in ASP.NET MVC are used to represent the business domain data.

In this chapter, you'll be learning about the following topics:

- Models and their purpose
- Creating a simple model and using it in the controller and views of the ASP.NET MVC application
- Creating a model specific to a View model
- Data flow in an ASP.NET MVC application in the context of models and `ViewModels`
- Purpose of the Entity Framework along with its features and benefits
- Adding, updating, and deleting data using the Entity Framework
- Using the Entity Framework in ASP.NET MVC applications

Models

Models are simple **POCO (Plain Old C# Objects)** classes representing your business domain data. For an e-commerce business, model classes would be `Product`, `Order`, and `Inventory`. If you are building an application for a university, model classes would be `Student`, `Teacher`, and `Subject`. Models represent the business domain data in your application and they are not aware of the underlying database that is being used in your application. In fact, you don't even need a database to work with models.

They can represent the data stored in an XML file or CSV file or any other data in your application. Having said that, these models could be used to interact with your database (in most cases) but they don't have any dependency to the database.

The following steps describe how to create an ASP.NET Core application that uses Models:

1. Make sure to create an ASP.NET 5 application with an empty template. Install the ASP.NET Core `NuGet` package and configure this, as discussed in an earlier chapter.
2. Create a `Controllers` folder and create a `HomeController` with a single `Index` action method.
3. Create the following folder/files for the `Views` model:

   - `Views`: This folder is inside your project.
   - `Views\_ViewStart.cshtml`: This identifies the name of the `Layout` file.
   - `Views\Shared` folder: This folder holds all the shared View components for your application.
   - `Shared\_Layout.cshtml`: This file identifies what your web application structure should look like.
   - `Views\Home` folder: This folder contains all of the Views of your `HomeController`.
   - `Views\Home\Index.cshtml`: This is the view corresponding to the `Index` action method of `HomeController`.

Now, we have created an ASP.NET Core application with Controllers and Views.

Let us create a `Models` folder in our application; this folder will contain all of your model files. In a real world application, this folder and the respective model files would reside in separate projects. For the sake of simplicity, we are keeping the `Models` folder and its files in the same project.

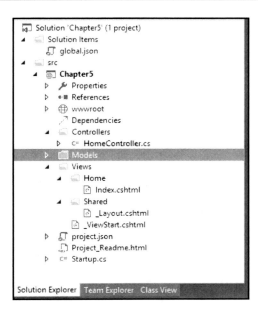

Let us create a simple model class `Product` model, in the `Models` folder:

```
public class Product {
  public int ProductId { get; set; }
  public string Name { get; set; }
  public decimal Price { get; set; }
}
```

This `Product` model class is no different from any other C# class and contains a few properties about the product.

Update the `Index` action method in `HomeController` to use the `Product` model, as shown in the following code snippet. We are building the model data and passing the model data to the View so that it can be shown to the users. However, it is *NOT* recommended to build the Model data in the controller's action methods as it violates the separation of concerns. For the sake of simplicity only, we are building the Model data in an action method.

```
public IActionResult Index() {
  /* Build the products model. It is NOT RECOMMENDED to build    models in
Controller action methods   like this. In real world appication, these
models and the     respective Data Access Layer(DAL) would   be in separate
projects. We are creating it here to make things    simpler to explain */
  List<Product> Products = new List<Product> {
    new Product {
      Name = "Mobile Phone",
      Price = 300
```

```
      },
      new Product {
        Name = "Laptop",
        Price = 1000
      },
      new Product {
        Name = "Tablet",
        Price = 600
      }
    };
    return View(Products);
}
```

Update the corresponding `Index` View method to use the Model data loop through each product and show it as an unordered list item. The `@model` in the first line represents the Model metadata; the type of data being passed to the View. The Model in the `for...each` loop represents the actual data itself, a list of products in our case:

```
@model List<Chapter5.Models.Product>

<ul>
  @foreach (var Product in Model) {
    <li>@Product.Name</li>
  }
</ul>
```

When you run the application, you'll get the following output:

We have successfully created a Model and have used it in our Controller and View.

Let us create a comparatively complex Model class, `Order` (`Order.cs` in the `Models` folder), which contains a list of products and their total amount:

```
public class Order {
  public int OrderId { get; set; }
  public List<Product> Products { get; set; }
```

```
public decimal Total { get; set; }
}
```

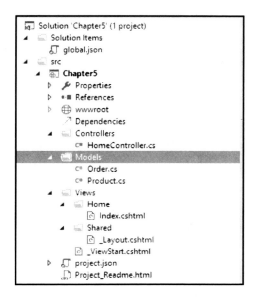

Now, we have to update the `Index` action method to use the `Order` model. Once we build the list of products, we are assigning the products list to the `Order` property and calculating the total cost of the order. These calculations would usually be done as part of the business layer. Again, for the sake of simplicity, we are building the data Model and calculations here in the action; this should never be the case in a real world application.

The code highlighted in bold is the changes that we have made in the action method:

```
public IActionResult Index() {
  /* Build the products model. It is NOT RECOMMENDED to build    models in
Controller action methods  like this. In real world appication, these
models and the    respective Data Access Layer(DAL) would  be in separate
projects. We are creating it here to make things    simpler to explain    */
  List<Product> Products = new List<Product> {
    new Product {
      Name = "Mobile Phone",
      Price = 300
    },
    new Product {
      Name = "Laptop",
      Price = 1000
    },
    new Product {
```

```
        Name = "Tablet",
        Price = 600
      }
  };

  Order order = new Order();
  order.Products = Products;
  order.Total = Products.Sum(product => product.Price);

  return View(order);
}
```

The View is updated to accommodate the Model changes. Model metadata (@model) is changed to indicate that the Order information is passed to the View instead of the list of products.

Then, we are showing the list of products in table format. Please note that all of the Model data (Order object and its properties, in this case) can be accessed through the Model. For example, the Products class can be accessed through Model.Products and the value of the Total can be obtained through Model.Total:

```
@model Chapter5.Models.Order

<table border="1">

  <tr>
    <th>Product Name</th>
    <th>Price</th>
  </tr>

  @foreach (var Product in Model.Products){
    <tr>
      <td>@Product.Name</td>
      <td>@Product.Price</td>
    </tr>
  }
  <tr>
    <td><b>Total</b></td>
    <td><b>@Model.Total</b></td>
  </tr>
</table>
```

When you run the application, you'll see the following output:

Models specific to a View component

There are scenarios where you might want to update only a few properties in a large Model or you might want to create a new Model based on a few models. In such scenarios, it is better to create a new Model specific to the View.

For example, let us assume that we are building a screen where you update the price of the product. This simple screen may contain only three properties—product ID, product name, and price of the product. But the product's Model may contain more than 30 properties to hold all details of the product such as manufacturer, color, size, and other properties. Instead of sending the complete Model with all the properties, we can create a new Model specific to this view with only a few properties—ID, Name, and Price.

Note on ViewModels

The ViewModels are entities where when you update the Model, your View would get updated automatically and vice versa. In many online articles and even in some books, they are referring to *ViewModels* when they are actually trying to mean *Models specific to the View*.

In ViewModels, binding is two ways—when you update either the Model or the View, the other one would get updated automatically. Let us consider a simple example; you have a form with various fields on the left-hand side and print preview on the right side. In this case, whatever you type in real time in the form will be reflected immediately on the right side. In such cases, you can use pure View models when you type, your ViewModel would be updated and that `ViewModel` would be consumed in the right-hand side print preview. These pure ViewModels are being used in advanced JavaScript frameworks such as **Knockout** or **AngularJS**.

In *Models specific to the View*, we are binding in only one way from the Model to the View. Here, we are sending a Model specific to the View instead of the generic Model (which represents a business domain class).

However, in this book, we will be referring to *Models specific to View* as `ViewModel` for brevity. Unless otherwise specified, you should read all ViewModels as *Models specific to View*. So, I am making the same mistake made by other authors ☺.

Data flow with respect to a Model

The following block diagram shows the data flow in an ASP.NET MVC application:

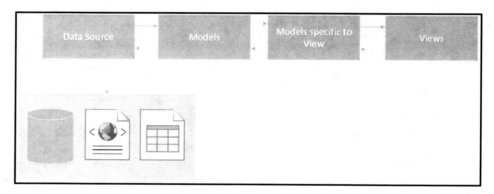

Data Source represents your application data. The application data could reside anywhere—from full-fledged RDBMS such as SQL servers to simple Excel spreadsheets, or anything in between.

Models represent the business domain data for your application and are independent of the data source being used. The same model could be used with different data sources.

We can use the **Model as-is in our views** to get data or to present it. But in some views, you might not need all the properties of the model. So, instead of sending the entire Model to the View, we create models specific to the View and use them in our View. This makes things simpler.

The following is the high-level sequence of events that happens when you store or retrieve a record in ASP.NET Core using the Model:

1. Users enter the data in a form (created using Views) in the application. The fields in the form do not need to represent the complete model as we need only a few properties in the Model.
2. The entered data is passed to the controller where Model binding happens. Model binding is the process where the data entered in the View gets mapped to the Model or ViewModel.
3. If the data is received in the ViewModel, then we would be converting the ViewModel to the Model.
4. Finally, the Model data is stored in the data source.

Till now, we have been handling only in-memory data in our application. In almost all real world applications, some form of the database will be used for data storage, access, and retrieval. In the next section, we will discuss the Entity Framework (ORM framework), which makes data access simpler from a .NET application.

Model binding

Model binding is the process of mapping the Model data coming from the View to the ViewModel parameter of the action method in the Controller.

Let us consider a simple form with a couple of form fields—Name and EmailID. On the submission of the form, these values would be mapped to the ViewModel object of the action method of the Controller. Model binding takes care of this mapping. The Model binder looks for a match in the form fields, query strings, and request parameters.

In the preceding example, any class with these properties would be picked up by ModelBinder without any issues.

As the following Person class contains the Name and EmailID properties, the model binder would not complain about using this model for mapping the entered values in the form:

```
public class Person {
    public string Name { get; set; }
    public string EmailID { get; set; }
}
```

The following code snippet shows how to use the `Person` class in the action method:

```
public ActionResult Add(Person p) {
  return View();
}
```

The Entity Framework

The Entity Framework is the **Object Relational Mapping (ORM)** framework that enables developers to work on domain-specific objects directly for data access instead of working on database queries. This reduces a lot of the code complexity in the data access layer in the application.

Before discussing the Entity Framework and its features, let us pause for a moment and think about the steps that we follow when we try to save some information to the database when using ADO.NET:

1. Construct the business domain object.
2. Create a connection to your database.
3. Open the connection.
4. Create a command object along with the command type.
5. Add the properties of your business domain object to the parameters of the command object.
6. Execute the command that saves the data into the database.

We have to follow the previously mentioned six steps for common operations such as saving a piece of data into the database.

If you are using an ORM framework such as the Entity Framework, you just need three steps:

1. Construct the business domain object.
2. Create the `DbContext` class for your business domain object. The instance of the `DbContext` class represents the session with the database.
3. Save it to the database using the instance of the `DBContext` class.

You might wonder how that is possible.

As a matter of fact, in the background, the Entity Framework creates a connection to the database and executes the query to save the business domain object to the database. To make it simple, the Entity Framework writes all the data access code for you so that you can concentrate on achieving the business functionality of the application rather than writing the database layer code.

The Entity Framework is independent of ASP.NET MVC

As discussed earlier, the Entity Framework is an ORM framework for accessing data and is independent of ASP.NET MVC. The Entity Framework could be used in **Windows Communication Foundation (WCF)** services, Web API services, and even in console applications. You could use the Entity Framework in any type of application and make use of it to access data using objects. The concepts and the functionalities of the Entity Framework remain the same, irrespective of the type of application that you use it with.

Now, we are going to use the Entity Framework with the console application. This allows us to concentrate on the task at hand and demonstrate the functionalities of the Entity Framework instead of working on the boilerplate code of the ASP.NET Core application. In a later part of this chapter, we will integrate the Entity Framework with the ASP.NET Core application.

The latest version of the Entity Framework for the SQL server is 7.0.0 and it is still in beta at the time of writing this book. EF7 (Entity Framework 7) brings significant changes when compared to its previous version (Entity Framework 6). However, EF7 is the recommended version when building ASP.NET 5 applications and hence we will be using this version in this book.

We need a database to explain many of the features of the Entity Framework. Please install SQL Server 2014 Express on your PC before continuing further. Step by step instructions for installing SQL Server 2014 Express and SQL Server Management Studio is given in *Appendix A*.

Creating console applications with the Entity Framework

Follow these steps to create a simple console application:

1. Select **File** | **New Project** and select **Console Application**.
2. Name the project and click on **OK**.

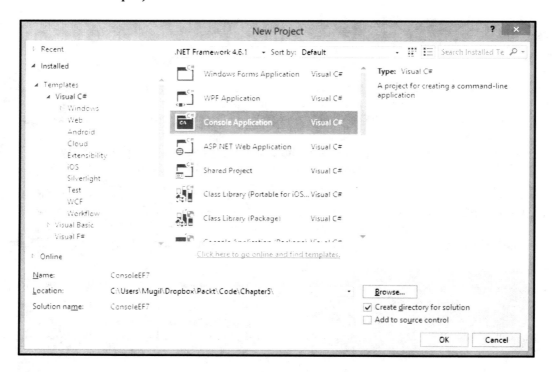

Installing the Entity Framework 7 NuGet package

There are two ways to install any NuGet package in your application:

- Using the NuGet Package Manager
- Using Package Manager Console

Using the NuGet Package Manager

People who prefer graphical interfaces can use this option:

1. Right-click on the console project and select **Manage NuGet Packages** from the context menu:

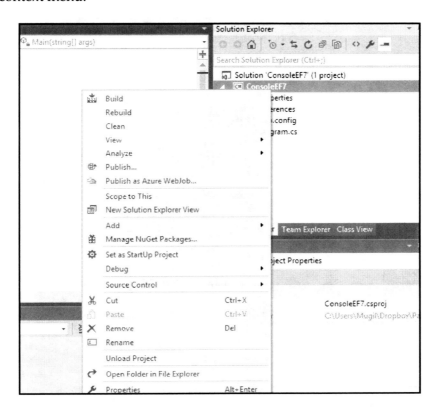

2. Search for `EntityFramework.MicrosoftSqlServer` in the `NuGet` package and make sure the **Include prerelease** checkbox is checked. Click on **Install** once you select **EntityFramework.MicrosoftSqlServer** and select **Latest pre-release 7.0.0-rc1-final** (at the time of writing this book). You can select any latest version of Entity Framework 7:

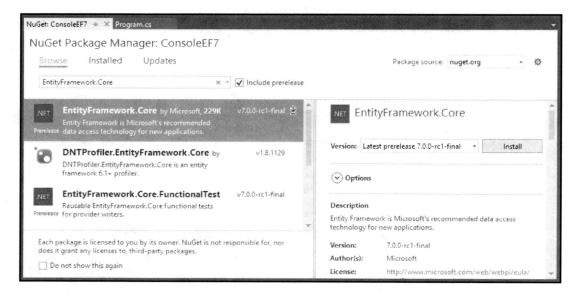

3. Once you click on **Install**, the `NuGet` package manager will ask you to review the changes. Click on **OK**:

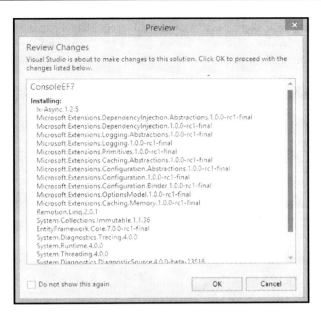

4. Click on **I Accept** in the **License Acceptance** window:

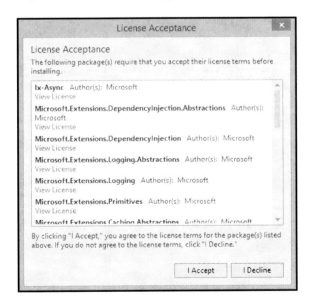

5. Once you click on **I Accept**, it will install the Entity Framework with all its dependencies. In the **Output** window, you will get the **Finished** message once the installation is complete:

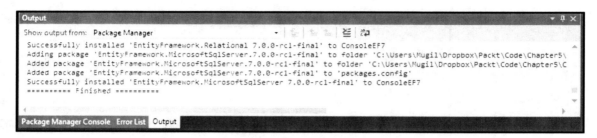

Using the Package Manager Console

To install the NuGet package using the Package Manager Console, follow these steps:

1. Open the **Package Manager Console** window by selecting the menu option **View | Other Windows | Package Manager Console**.

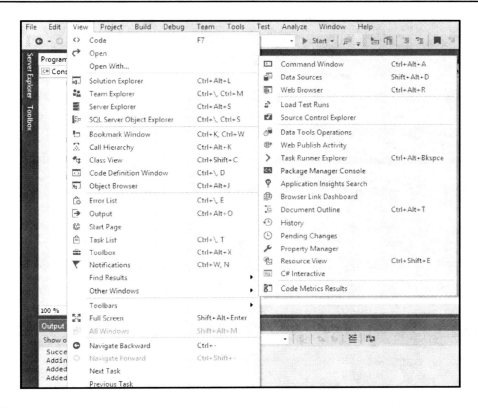

2. Type `Install-Package EntityFramework.MicrosoftSqlServer - Pre` in the **Package Manager Console** window as shown in the following screenshot:

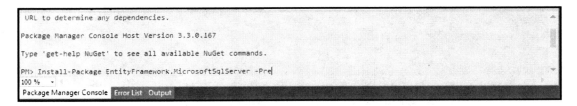

3. Once the installation is complete, a message, **Successfully installed 'EntityFramework.MicrosoftSqlServer 7.0.0-rc1-final'**, will be shown:

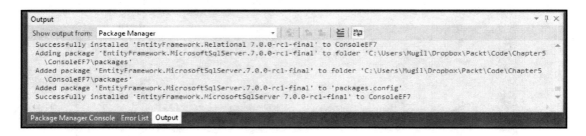

Installing Entity Framework commands

We need to install the Entity Framework commands package in order to perform migration activities. Migration includes the creation of a database and its associated tables. Any changes in the schema will also be taken care of by migration:

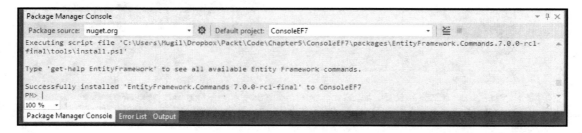

As discussed earlier, we need to follow three steps in order to interact with the database when we are using the Entity Framework:

1. Create the `Model` classes.
2. Create the `DbContext` class for your business domain object. The instance of the `DbContext` class represents the session with the database.
3. Construct the business domain object and save it to the database using the instance of the `DBContext` class.

Let us discuss each of the preceding steps in details and try to save an object to the database.

Creating Model classes

The `Model` classes are simple POCO objects, which can be used with the Entity Framework.

Let us create a POCO class for our business domain object, the `Employee` class in our case. I have created a new file named `Employee.cs` in our console application with the following content. This `Employee` class contains a few properties of an employee and has no special properties or fields to make it work with the Entity Framework.

Let's take a look at the following code snippet:

```
public class Employee {
  public int EmployeeId { get; set; }
  public string Name { get; set; }
  public decimal Salary { get; set; }
  public string Designation { get; set; }
}
```

By convention, if the property name is `Id` or `ClassName+Id`, it will be considered as a primary key by Entity Framework while creating the database table.

Properties with string data types will be created as fields of the type `nvarchar(max)`. However, we can override this behavior by using annotations, which we will be discussed later.

Creating the DbContext class

The instance of the `DbContext` class represents the session to the database and this `DbContext` class does most of the heavy lifting of your data access for your application.

Create a new class by the named `EmployeeDbContext` with the following content:

```
using Microsoft.Data.Entity;
using System.Configuration;

namespace ConsoleEF7 {
  public class EmployeeDbContext : DbContext{
    public DbSet<Employee> Employees {get; set;}

    protected override void OnConfiguring(DbContextOptionsBuilder
optionsBuilder) {string connectionString =
ConfigurationManager.ConnectionStrings
["SqlServerExpress"].ConnectionString;
      optionsBuilder.UseSqlServer(connectionString);
      base.OnConfiguring(optionsBuilder);
```

```
      }
    }
  }
```

Configure it using `App.Config`:

```xml
<?xml version="1.0" encoding="utf-8" ?>
<configuration>
  <startup>
    <supportedRuntime version="v4.0"
    sku=".NETFramework,Version=v4.6.1" />
  </startup>
  <connectionStrings>
    <add name="SqlServerExpress" connectionString="Data Source=    MUGIL-
PC\SQLEXPRESS;Initial Catalog=EF7Console;Integrated    Security=True"/>
  </connectionStrings>
</configuration>
```

There are a few things to be noted in the preceding code snippet:

- **Include the** `Microsoft.Data.Entity` **namespace as the** `DbContext` **class available in this namespace. Our connection string is available in the** `App.Config` **file. In order to read the contents of the** `App.Config` **file, we are including the** `ConfigurationManager` **class in** `System.Configuration`.
- **In order to use the** `DbContext` **API, a class has to be created which inherits from the** `DbContext` **class so that we can access methods of the** `DbContext` **API. We have created the** `EmployeeDbContext` **class which was inherited from** `DbContext` **class.**
- `DbSet` **is a class which allows operations of the Entity Framework to be performed for a given Entity type. We need to create the** `DbSet` **object for each of the Entity types that we use in our application. In this example, we are using only one** `DbSet` **object as we are working with the** `Employee` **class.**

Create a migration

Migration is the process of recording all the changes of your database. `Add-Migration` is the Entity Framework command for adding migration:

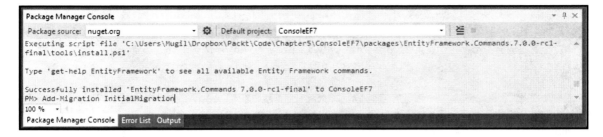

1. Once you add the migration, you can revoke the changes by executing the `Remove-Migration` **Entity Framework command.**

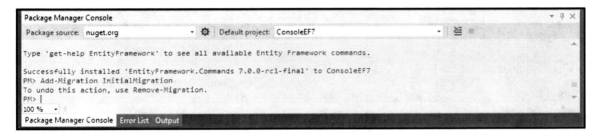

- This is what the migrations directory looks like:

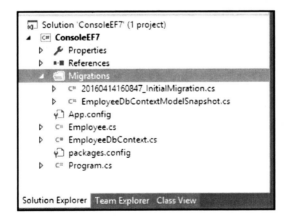

2. Update the database by issuing the Entity Framework command `Update-Database`, which updates the database tables as per the information available in the migration. As we have installed the `EntityFramework.Commands` package earlier, these commands will be available for the application:

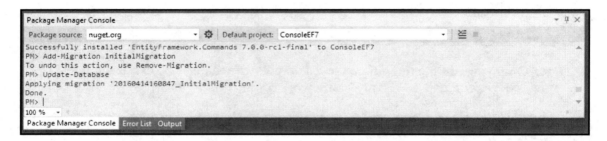

3. Once you update the database, you can see the changes in the database by connecting to SQL Server Management Studio:

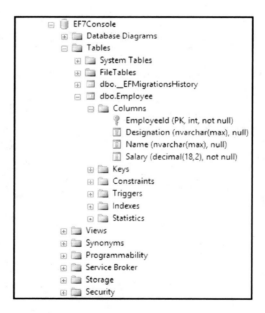

4. Perform the database operation to save the business domain object in the database. You can create the database manually or, if the database is not available, it will create one for you.

The `Main` method is updated with the following code:

```
class Program {
  static void Main(string[] args) {
    AddEmployee();
  }

  static void AddEmployee() {
    using (var db = new EmployeeDbContext()) {
      Employee employee= new Employee {
        Designation = "Software Engineer",
        Name = "Scott",
        Salary = 5600
      };

      db.Employees.Add(employee);
      int recordsInserted = db.SaveChanges();
      Console.WriteLine("Number of records inserted:" +
recordsInserted);
      Console.ReadLine();
    }
  }
}
```

Firstly, we are constructing the business domain object. Then, we are adding the constructed `Employee` object to the employee's `DbSet` of the `DbContext` class. Finally, we are calling the `SaveChanges` method `DbContext` API, which will save all the pending changes to the database.

You might be wondering how it can save it to the database when we have not even given the connection string.

Let us discuss what happens behind the scenes when we run the program:

- When you make changes to any of the `DbSet` collection, the Entity Framework checks whether the database exists. If it does not exist, it creates a new one using the pattern `<Namespace of DbContextName>`. In our case, a database called by `EF6.EmployeeDbContext` would be created.
- Then, it creates database tables for the entities declared in `DbSet`. By convention, the Entity Framework uses the pluralized form of Entity for the table names. As we have declared `DbSet` for the `Employee` entity, the Entity Framework creates a pluralized form of `Employee` and creates the table named `Employees`.

The creation of the database and tables happens when the following code is executed:

```
db.Employees.Add(employee);
```

When `SaveChanges` method is executed, the data in the `Employee` object will get saved to the database and returns the number of records affected. In the preceding case, it returns `1`.

When you run the application again, the first two steps mentioned previously will be skipped as the database and table will have already been created.

When you query the database, you can see the newly inserted record:

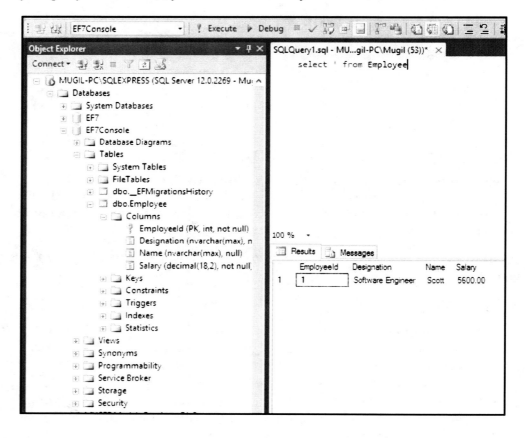

How the SaveChanges method works

When we are making changes, the Entity Framework tracks the state of each of the objects and executes the appropriate query when SaveChanges method is called.

For example, when we add an Employee object to the employees' collection (DbSet), this object is being tracked as Entity in the Added state. When SaveChanges is called, the Entity Framework creates an insert query for the same and executes it. The same is the case with updating and deleting the object. The Entity Framework sets the Entity state of the respective objects to Modified and Deleted. When SaveChanges is called, it creates and executes the Update and Delete queries.

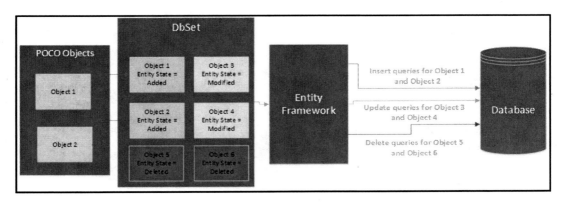

The preceding figure explains how the SaveChanges method works at a high-level for different types of change. We have a couple of POCO objects (**Object 1** and **Object 2**), which have been added to the employees' DbSet object. Let us assume **Object 3** and **Object 4** have been modified and objects **Object 5** and **Object 6** are in Deleted state. When you call SaveChanges method, it creates three sets of queries. The first set of queries is for the addition of objects, resulting in insert queries getting executed against the database. In the second set of queries, Update queries are created and executed for the objects whose state is modified. Finally, Delete queries are executed for the objects for all the Deleted state objects.

Updating the record

Let us try to update the salary of an inserted employee record using the Entity Framework:

```
static void UpdateSalary() {
  using (var db = new EmployeeDbContext()){
```

```
    Employee employee = db.Employees.Where(emp => emp.EmployeeId        ==
1).FirstOrDefault();
    if(employee!=null){
      employee.Salary = 6500;
      int recordsUpdated = db.SaveChanges();
      Console.WriteLine("Records updated:" + recordsUpdated);
      Console.ReadLine();
    }
  }
}
```

In the preceding method, we find the employee with `EmployeeId` = 1. Then, we update the salary of the employee to `6500` and save the `employee` object to the database. Please note that, in the preceding method, we interact with the database a couple of times—once to find the correct employee record (`read` operation) and again to update the record (`update` operation).

```
static void Main(string[] args){
  UpdateSalary();
}
```

The `Main` method is updated to call the `UpdateSalary` method. When you query the database, you should see the record with the updated information:

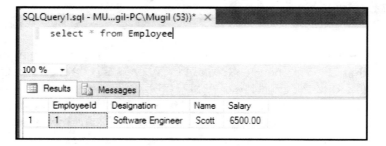

Deleting the record

Deleting the record is a bit tricky as it involves setting the state directly. In the following method, firstly we get the object and setting the state of the object to `Deleted`. Then calling the `SaveChanges` method will generate the `delete` query for the object and execute it, which in turn will eventually delete the record in the database:

```
static void DeleteEmployee() {
  using (var db = new EmployeeDbContext()) {
    Employee employeeToBeDeleted = db.Employees.Where(emp =>
```

```
emp.EmployeeId == 1).FirstOrDefault();
    if (employeeToBeDeleted != null) {
        db.Entry(employeeToBeDeleted).State =
Microsoft.Data.Entity.EntityState.Deleted;
        int recordsDeleted = db.SaveChanges();
        Console.WriteLine("Number of records deleted:" +
recordsDeleted);
        Console.ReadLine();
    }
  }
}

static void Main(string[] args) {
  DeleteEmployee();
}
```

Using the Entity Framework in ASP.NET MVC applications

There is not much difference between using the Entity Framework in a console application and ASP.NET MVC application. Now, we are going to build a simple application with a single screen as shown in the following image. In this screen, we will have a form where the user will enter the information about the employee; once the user submits the form, the information will be saved to the database and reflected in the following screenshots:

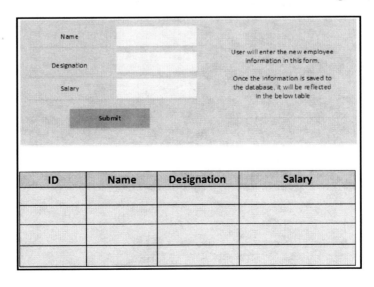

We can create a simple Model for the employee. We need to build a ViewModel for this View, as we need to get the employee information from the user and we need to show a list of employees as well on the same screen.

Let us create an ASP.NET Core application, adding the employee and showing the list of employees. The following is the step-by-step instructions to create the application for the previously mentioned objective:

1. Create an ASP.NET Core project in Visual Studio by selecting an empty ASP.NET 5 application.
2. Install the ASP.NET Core `NuGet` package.
3. Install the Entity Framework 7 `NuGet` package and **ef** EntityFramework commands (for database migration) as explained earlier in this chapter.
4. Add `config.json` to declare the connection string of the database:

```
{
  "Data": {
    "DefaultConnection": {
      "ConnectionString": "Data Source=MUGIL-PC\\SQLEXPRESS;Initial
Catalog=Validation;Integrated Security=True"
    }
  }
}
```

5. Update `project.json` to include EntityFramework 7 and EntityFramework commands. The changes are highlighted in bold:

```
{
  "version": "1.0.0-*",
  "compilationOptions":{
    "emitEntryPoint": true
  },

  "dependencies": {
    "Microsoft.AspNet.IISPlatformHandler":      "1.0.0-rc1-final",
    "Microsoft.AspNet.Mvc": "6.0.0-rc1-final",
    "Microsoft.AspNet.Server.Kestrel": "1.0.0-rc1-final",
    "EntityFramework.MicrosoftSqlServer":       "7.0.0-rc1-final",
    "EntityFramework.Commands": "7.0.0-rc1-final"
  },

  "commands": {
    "web": "Microsoft.AspNet.Server.Kestrel",
    "ef": "EntityFramework.Commands"
  },
```

```
"frameworks": {
  "dnx451": { },
  "dnxcore50": { }
},

"exclude": [
  "wwwroot",
  "node_modules"
],
"publishExclude": [
  "**.user",
  "**.vspscc"
]
}
```

6. Configure MVC in the `Startup` class (`Startup.cs`):

- In the constructor, we are building the configuration by reading the `config.json` file
- Add the MVC service and the Entity Framework service to the services in the `ConfigureServices` method
- Configure the MVC routing in the `Configure` method:

```
using Microsoft.AspNet.Builder;
using Microsoft.AspNet.Hosting;
using Microsoft.AspNet.Http;
using Microsoft.Extensions.DependencyInjection;
using Microsoft.Extensions.Configuration;
using Validation.Models;
using Microsoft.Data.Entity;
using Microsoft.Extensions.PlatformAbstractions;

namespace Validation {
 public class Startup {
 public IConfigurationRoot Configuration { get; set; }

public Startup(IHostingEnvironment env, IApplicationEnvironment appEnv) {
 var builder = new ConfigurationBuilder()
 .AddJsonFile("config.json")
 .AddEnvironmentVariables();
 Configuration = builder.Build();
 }

// This method gets called by the runtime. Use this method to add services
to the container.
// For more information on how to configure your application, visit http
```

```
://go.microsoft.com/fwlink/?LinkID=398940

public void ConfigureServices(IServiceCollection services) {
services.AddEntityFramework()
 .AddSqlServer()
 .AddDbContext<EmployeeDbContext>(options => {
 options.UseSqlServer(Configuration.Get<string>
("Data:DefaultConnection:ConnectionString"));
 });
 services.AddMvc();
 }
// This method gets called by the runtime. Use this method to configure the
HTTP request pipeline.

public void Configure(IApplicationBuilder app) {
 app.UseIISPlatformHandler();
 app.UseMvc(routes => {
 routes.MapRoute(
 name: "default",
 template: "{controller=Employee}/ {action=Index}/{id?}");
 });
 }
// Entry point for the application.
 public static void Main(string[] args) =>
WebApplication.Run<Startup>(args);
 }
 }
```

7. **Create** `Models` **and** `DbContext` **classes.**

8. **Create the** `Models` **folder and add the** `Employee` **model class and** `EmployeeDbContext` **class.**

9. **Create the** `Employee` **Model class** (`Employee.cs` **in the** `Models` **folder):**

```
public class Employee {
  public int EmployeeId { get; set; }
  public string Name { get; set; }
  public string Designation { get; set; }
  public decimal Salary { get; set; }
}
```

10. **Create** `EmployeeDbContext` (`EmployeeDbContext.cs` **in the** `Models` **folder):**

```
using Microsoft.Data.Entity;
using Microsoft.Extensions.Configuration;
```

```
namespace Validation.Models {
  public class EmployeeDbContext : DbContext {

    public IConfigurationRoot Configuration { get; set; }

    public DbSet<Employee> Employees { get; set; }

    public EmployeeDbContext() {
      var builder = new ConfigurationBuilder()
      .AddJsonFile("config.json")
      .AddEnvironmentVariables();
      Configuration = builder.Build();
    }

    protected override void OnConfiguring     (DbContextOptionsBuilder
optionsBuilder) {        optionsBuilder.UseSqlServer
(Configuration.Get<string>
("Data:DefaultConnection:ConnectionString"));
      base.OnConfiguring(optionsBuilder);
    }
  }
}
```

11. **Create** `ViewModels`:

- As we are going to show a list of employees and the form to add employees in the same screen, we are going to build a Model specific to this View. This model will contain information about the list of employees and the employee to be added.

12. **Create the** `ViewModels` **folder and add the** `EmployeeAddViewModel`:

```
using MVCEF7.Models;

namespace MVCEF7.ViewModels {
  public class EmployeeAddViewModel {
    public List<Employee> EmployeesList { get; set; }
    public Employee NewEmployee { get; set; }
  }
}
```

- This `ViewModel` has a couple of properties. `EmployeesList` and `NewEmployee`. `EmployeesList` will contain the list of employees. This list would be fetched from the database. `NewEmployee` will hold the employee information entered by the user.

13. **Create** `Controllers` **to handle the incoming requests:**

- **Create a** `Controllers` **folder and add the** `EmployeeController` **class with a couple of action methods-one for** `GET` **and another for** `POST`**. The** `Index` **action method corresponding to the** `GET` **action method will be called when you access the URL** (`http://localhost/Employee/Index`) **or when you run the application. The** `POST` `Index` **action method will be called when you submit the form as following:**

```
public IActionResult Index() {
  EmployeeAddViewModel employeeAddViewModel = new
EmployeeAddViewModel();
  using (var db = new EmployeeDbContext()) {
    employeeAddViewModel.EmployeesList =        db.Employees.ToList();
    employeeAddViewModel.NewEmployee = new Employee();

  }
  return View(employeeAddViewModel);
}
```

- **In the preceding** `GET` `Index` **action method, we are creating the** `ViewModel` **object and passing it to the View.**
- **The following code uses** `POST` `Index` **action method:**

```
[HttpPost]
public IActionResult Index(EmployeeAddViewModel  employeeAddViewModel) {

  using (var db = new EmployeeDbContext()) {
    db.Employees.Add(employeeAddViewModel.NewEmployee);
    db.SaveChanges();
    //Redirect to get Index GET method
    return RedirectToAction("Index");
  }

}
```

- **We get the** `NewEmployee` **property in the ViewModel, which contains the information on the user. Save it to the database. Once we save the employee information to the database and we redirect the control to the** `GET` `Index` **action method, the** `GET` `Index` **action method will again show the form to enter the employee information and the list of employees in table format.**

14. Add the `Views` folder:

1. **Create** `Views\_ViewStart.cshtml` **with the following content:**

```
@{
  Layout = "_Layout";
}
```

2. **Create** `Views\Shared\_Layout.cshtml` **with the following content:**

```html
<!DOCTYPE html>

<html>
  <head>
    <meta name="viewport" content="width=device-width" />
    <title>@ViewBag.Title</title>
  </head>
  <body>
    <div>
      @RenderBody()
    </div>
  </body>
</html>
```

3. **Create** `Views\Employee\Index.cshtml` **with the following content:**

```
@model MVCEF.ViewModels.EmployeeAddViewModel
@*
//For more information on enabling MVC for empty projects,  visit
http://go.microsoft.com/fwlink/?LinkID=397860
*@
@{
}

<div>
  @using (Html.BeginForm("Index", "Employee",    FormMethod.Post)) {
    <table>
      <tr>
        <td>@Html.LabelFor(Model =>          Model.NewEmployee.Name)</td>
        <td>@Html.TextBoxFor(Model =>         Model.NewEmployee.Name)</td>
      </tr>
      <tr>
        <td>@Html.LabelFor(Model =>
Model.NewEmployee.Designation)</td>
        <td>@Html.TextBoxFor(Model =>
Model.NewEmployee.Designation)</td>
      </tr>
      <tr>
```

```
        <td>@Html.LabelFor(Model =>            Model.NewEmployee.Salary)</td>
        <td>@Html.TextBoxFor(Model =>
Model.NewEmployee.Salary)</td>
      </tr>
      <tr>
        <td colspan="2"><input type="submit"          value="Submit"/>
        </td>
      </tr>
    </table>

  }
</div>

<br/><br/> <br/>

<b> List of employees:</b> <br/>
<div>
  <table border="1">
    <tr>
      <th> ID </th>
      <th> Name </th>
      <th> Designation </th>
      <th> Salary </th>
    </tr>
    @foreach(var employee in Model.EmployeesList) {
      <tr>
        <td>@employee.EmployeeId</td>
        <td>@employee.Name</td>
        <td>@employee.Designation</td>
        <td>@employee.Salary</td>
      </tr>
    }
  </table>
</div>
```

In the preceding `Index` view, we create a form where we get the employee information from the user in the topmost `div`. In the next `div`, we show the list of employees in a tabular format.

Once we create all the folders and the files, the project structure should look like the following:

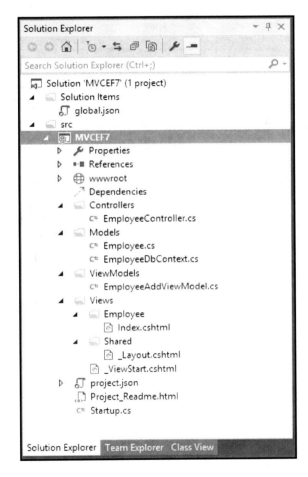

Database migration

We have created the business entity—the `Employee` class. Now, we can proceed with the migration. Migration is a two-step process: in the first step, we create the migration files. This can be done by executing the following command from the command prompt from the context of the project:

```
dnx ef migrations add InitialMigration
```

This command will create the migration files in your project, as shown in the following screenshot:

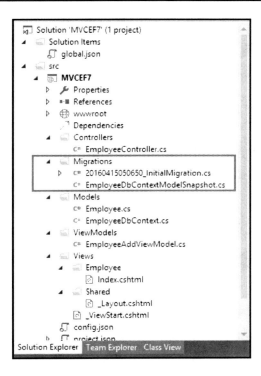

Then execute the following command to create the database:

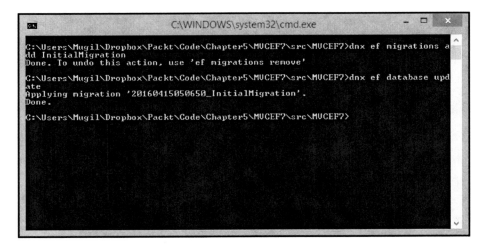

This command will read the migration files created in the previous step and create the database along with the associated tables:

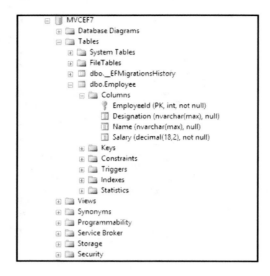

Run the application. You will get the following screen, where the user can enter the employee information in the form. As we are using the strongly typed model in our view, it takes the default values for all the properties. The Name and Designation are properties of type string and the default values are empty string for these fields, Salary is of type decimal and the default value for decimal is 0 hence 0 is shown in the form when it is loaded for the Salary field.

As there are no records, we are showing 0 records in the List of employees table:

When you enter the information in the form and submit it, the information gets saved in the database and all the database records in the `Employees` table will be presented as follows:

Summary

In this chapter, we learned what a Model is and how it fits in the ASP.NET MVC application. Then, we created a simple Model, built model data in a Controller, passed the Model to the View, and shown the data using the View. We have learned about the *Models specific to a View* and have discussed the flow of the data with respect to Models. We learned about the Entity Framework, an ORM framework from Microsoft, and how it simplifies database access from your .NET application. We have created simple console application where we have inserted, updated, and deleted the records. Finally, we have built an ASP.NET Core application that uses Model, ViewModel, and Entity Framework.

6
Validation

We can never rely on the data entered by users. Sometimes they might be ignorant about the application and thus they may be entering incorrect data unknowingly. At other times, some malign users may want to corrupt the application by entering inappropriate data into it. In either case, we need to validate the input data before storing the data for further processing.

In this chapter, you'll be learning about the following topics:

- Different types of validation
- Server-side validation with an example
- Client-side validation with an example
- Unobtrusive JavaScript validation using jQuery unobtrusive libraries, where we don't have to write separate code for validation

In an ideal case, users will enter valid data in a proper format in your application. But, as you might realize, the real world is not so ideal. Users will enter incorrect data in your application. As a developer, it is the responsibility of us to validate the user input in our application. If the entered input is not valid, you need to inform the user, saying what has gone wrong, so that the user can correct the input data and submit the form again.

Validation can be done on the client-side or the server-side or at both ends. If the validation is done before sending the data to the server, it is called client-side validation. For example, if the user does not enter any data in a mandatory field, we can validate (by finding the data that is not entered) the form, at the client-side itself. There is no need to send the form data to the server. JavaScript is the most commonly used language being used for client-side validation.

If the validation is done at the server-side (sending the form data to the server), it is called server-side validation. For instance, you might want to validate data entered by the user against the data in the database. In this case, it is preferable to do server-side validation as we cannot have all the data in the database at the client-side.

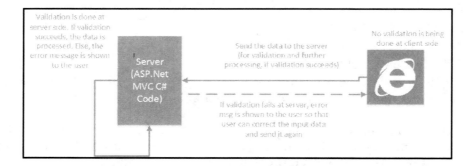

Client-side and server-side validation

In the real world, it's not a case of either server-side or client-side validation. We can have both types of validation at the same time. In fact, it is recommended to validate the data at both ends to avoid unnecessary processing.

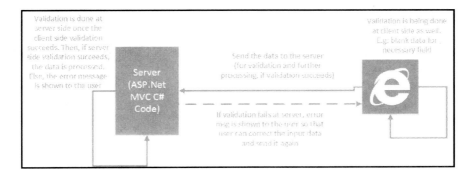

The preceding figure shows the validation is being performed at both the client-side and the server-side. If the data is not entered into the required field, we can catch that issue at the client-side itself. There is no need to send the data to the server to finally find out that there is no data entered. Once all the required data is entered, the data is sent back to the server to validate the entered data based on some business logic. If the validation fails, the form data is sent again to the browser with the error message so that the user can send the data again.

We have covered enough theory about the need for validation and the types of validations typically used in the application. Let us get our hands dirty by adding validation to the application that we built in the previous chapter.

The following screenshot is the form that we have built in the previous chapter. There is nothing fancy in this form—just three fields. When a user enters the data in the form, the data is stored in the database and the entire employee information is fetched back and shown in a tabular format.

In the existing application that we have built, we do not show any message to the user even when the user does not enter any information in any of the fields and submits it. Instead, we silently store the default values for the fields (empty values for string types and 0.00 for decimal types) as shown in the following screenshot:

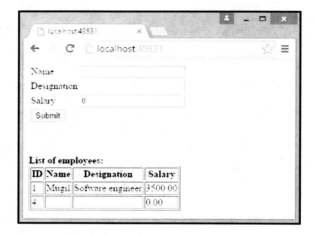

But this should not be the case. We should inform the user saying that the data entered is not valid and ask the user to correct the input data.

Server-side validation

Let us continue with the application that we built in the previous chapter. To do server-side validation, we need to do the following:

1. Add Data Annotation attributes to the `ViewModels` model class. The input data is validated against this metadata and the model state is updated automatically.
2. Update the `view` method to display the validation message for each of the fields. The `span` tag helper with the `asp-validation-for` attribute will be used to display the validation error message.
3. Update the controller action method to verify the model state. If the model state is valid, we insert the data into the database. Otherwise, the View model is updated and the `view` method is rendered again with the validation error message so that the user can update with valid input data and submit the form again.

Updating View models with the Data Annotation attribute

The Data Annotation attributes defines the validation rules for the properties of the `Model`/`ViewModel`. If the input data does not match with the attribute definition in the model, the validation will fail, which in turn makes the associated model state invalid.

There are several Data Annotation attributes available to validate the data. The following are the most commonly used Data Annotations attributes:

- **Required**: This attribute indicates the property is required.
- **Range**: This attribute defines the minimum and maximum constraints.
- **MinLength**: This defines the minimum length a property must have in order for the validation to succeed.
- **MaxLength**: As the name implies, this attribute defines the maximum length of the property. If the length of the property value exceeds the maximum length, the validation would fail.
- **RegularExpression**: We can use a regular expression for data validation if we use this attribute.

As Data Annotation attributes are available in the `System.ComponentModel.DataAnnotations` namespace, we need to include this namespace. The following is the updated View model code:

```
using System;
using System.Collections.Generic;
using System.ComponentModel.DataAnnotations;
using System.Linq;
using System.Threading.Tasks;
using Validation.Models;

namespace Validation.ViewModels
{
    public class EmployeeAddViewModel
    {
        public List<Employee> EmployeesList { get; set; }
        [Required(ErrorMessage ="Employee Name is required")]
        public string Name { get; set; }

        [Required(ErrorMessage ="Employee Designation is required")]
        [MinLength(5, ErrorMessage = "Minimum length of designation should
be 5 characters")]
        public string Designation { get; set; }
```

```
        [Required]
        [Range(1000,9999.99)]
        public decimal Salary { get; set; }
    }
}
```

We have added Data Annotation attributes for all the three properties—Name, Designation, and Salary.

The ErrorMessage attribute displays a message to be displayed when the validation fails. If there is a failure of validation and if there is no ErrorMessage mentioned, the default error message will be displayed.

Updating the View model to display the validation error message

For each of the fields, we have added a span tag where the error message is displayed in a red color when the validation fails. When the validation succeeds, there will be no error message displayed. The attribute value of asp-validation-for represents the field name for which the validation error message has to be displayed. For example, we have used the span tag with the asp-validation-for attribute and with the value Name, which tells ASP.NET MVC to display the validation error message for the Name field:

```
<form asp-controller="Employee" asp-action="Index">
    <table>
        <tr>
            <td><label asp-for="Name"></label></td>
            <td><input asp-for="Name" /></td>
            <td><span asp-validation-for="Name"
style="color:red"></span></td>
        </tr>
        <tr>
            <td><label asp-for="Designation"></label> </td>
            <td><input asp-for="Designation" /></td>
            <td><span asp-validation-for="Designation"
style="color:red"></span> </td>
        </tr>
        <tr>
            <td><label asp-for="Salary"></label></td>
            <td><input asp-for="Salary"></td>
            <td> <span asp-validation-for="Salary"
style="color:red"></span> </td>
        </tr>
        <tr>
```

```
                    <td colspan="2"><input type="submit" id="submitbutton"
value="Submit" /></td>
              </tr>
        </table>
     </form>
```

Updating the controller action method to verify the model state

The model state is automatically updated based on the Data Annotation attribute specified on our View model and the input data. We are verifying whether the model state is valid in the following `Index` method, which is a `POST` action method. If the model state is valid (when the validation succeeds), we save the entered data to the database. If the validation fails, then the `ModelState` is set to `invalid` automatically. Then, we would populate the `ViewModel` with the entered data and render the `View` method again so that the user can correct the input data and re-submit the data:

```
[HttpPost]
    public IActionResult Index(EmployeeAddViewModel employeeAddViewModel)
{
        if (ModelState.IsValid)
        {
            using (var db = new EmployeeDbContext())
            {
                Employee newEmployee = new Employee
                {
                    Name = employeeAddViewModel.Name,
                    Designation = employeeAddViewModel.Designation,
                    Salary = employeeAddViewModel.Salary
                };
                db.Employees.Add(newEmployee);
                db.SaveChanges();
                //Redirect to get Index GET method
                return RedirectToAction("Index");
            }
        }
        using (var db = new EmployeeDbContext())
        {
            employeeAddViewModel.EmployeesList = db.Employees.ToList();
        }
        return View(employeeAddViewModel);
    }
```

When you run the application after making aforementioned changes and submit the form without entering the values, error messages will be displayed beside the fields as shown in the following screenshot. Please note that, even in the case of a validation error, we display the employees' data in the following table, which is achieved by using the code block in the previous code snippet.

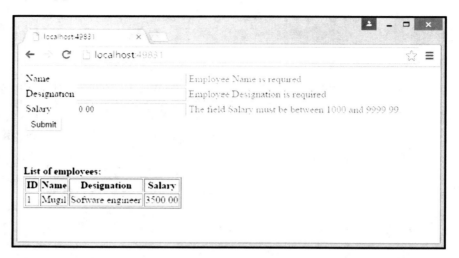

There are a few things to be noted in the previous validation and its error message:

- If the validation fails, error messages are displayed as expected.
- If there is more than one validation for a field, it will display one error message at a time. For example, we have a couple of validations for **Designation** field—the `Required` and `MinLength` attributes. If there is no data entered for the field, only the required field error message will be displayed. Only when the required field error is resolved (by entering some characters in the field), the second validation error message will be displayed.
- If no error message is available and if the validation fails, the default error message is displayed. We have not given any error message for the **Salary** field. So, when the validation fails for that field, ASP.NET MVC displays the default error message based on the field name and the type of validation failure.

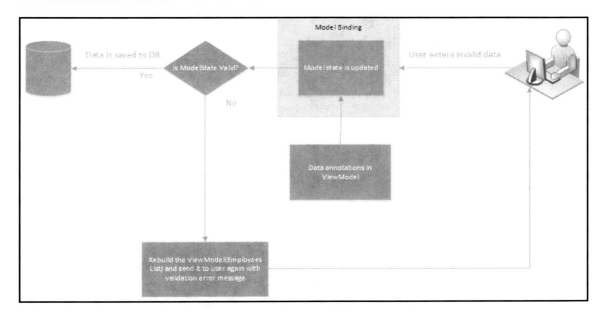

The preceding figure depicts the high-level sequence of events in server-side validation and is described as follows:

1. The user enters the invalid data.
2. Based on the Data Annotations attribute in the View model, the model state is updated automatically. This happens during the model binding process where the data in the `view` method is mapped to the data in the model or View model.
3. In the controller's action method, we are verifying the model state.
4. If the model state is valid, we are saving the entered data to the database.
5. If the model state is not valid, we are rending the View model again with the validation error message so that the user can correct the input data and submit the form again with the valid input data.

Client-side validation

There are scenarios where we don't need to go to the server to validate the input data. In the preceding example of the server-side validation, we do not need to go to the server to verify whether the user has entered the data for the **Name** field. We can validate at the client-side itself. This prevents round-trips to the server and reduces the server load.

We are going to use JavaScript to validate the data from the client-side. JavaScript is a high-level, interpreted language which is primarily used in client-side programming.

 These days, JavaScript is also being used at the server-side as part of Node.js.

We are going to make a couple of changes in our View model (`Index.cshtml` file) to validate the form at the client-side:

1. Changes in the form: add the `id` attribute to all the `span` tags so that we can access this HTML element to display the HTML error message. On submission of the form, call a JavaScript function to validate the input data.
2. Add the script HTML element and create a JavaScript function to validate the input data.

In the following code, we are calling the `validateForm` JavaScript function on submission of the form. If the `validateForm` function returns `true`, the data will be sent to the server. Otherwise, the data will not be sent. We have added the `id` attribute for all the `span` tags so that we can identify the `span` tags and display the validation error messages over there:

```
<form asp-controller="Employee" asp-action="Index" onsubmit="return
validateForm()">
        <table>
            <tr>
                <td><label asp-for="Name"></label></td>
                <td><input asp-for="Name" /></td>
                <td><span id="validationName" asp-validation-for="Name"
style="color:red"></span></td>
            </tr>
            <tr>
                <td><label asp-for="Designation"></label> </td>
                <td><input asp-for="Designation" /></td>
                <td><span id="validationDesignation" asp-validation-
for="Designation" style="color:red"></span> </td>
            </tr>
            <tr>
                <td><label asp-for="Salary"></label></td>
                <td><input asp-for="Salary"></td>
                <td> <span id="validationSalary" asp-validation-
for="Salary" style="color:red"></span> </td>
            </tr>
            <tr>
                <td colspan="2"><input type="submit" id="submitbutton"
```

```
value="Submit" /></td>
            </tr>
        </table>
</form>
```

We have added the JavaScript function to validate all three fields. We get the values of all the three fields and we store them in separate variables. Then we verify whether the value of each of the variables is null or empty. If the value is empty, we get the span element for the respective field and set the text context with the validation error message:

```
<script type="text/javascript">
        function validateForm() {
            var isValidForm = true;
            var nameValue = document.getElementById("Name").value;
            var designationValue =
document.getElementById("Designation").value;
            var salaryValue = document.getElementById("Salary").value;

            //Validate the name field
            if (nameValue == null || nameValue == "") {
                document.getElementById("validationName").textContent =
"Employee Name is required - from client side";
                isValidForm = false;
            }

            //validate the designation field
            if (designationValue == null || designationValue == "") {
document.getElementById("validationDesignation").textContent = "Employee
Designation is required - from client side";
                isValidForm = false;
            }

            //validate the salary field - if it is empty
            if (salaryValue == null || salaryValue == "") {
                document.getElementById("validationSalary").textContent =
"Employee Salary is required - from client side";
                isValidForm = false;
            }else if (Number(salaryValue) == NaN ||
Number(salaryValue)<=0.0) {
                document.getElementById("validationSalary").textContent =
"Please enter valid number for salary field - from client side";
                isValidForm = false;
            }


            return isValidForm;

        }
```

```
</script>
```

When you run the application and submit the form without entering the data, you'll get the error message generated from the client-side itself without ever going to the server.

In real-world applications, we would not be hand coding the validation code at the JavaScript. Instead, most applications use unobtrusive validation, where we do not write JavaScript code for validating each of the fields. Simply adding the respective JavaScript libraries will do.

You might wonder how the fields get validated without ever writing the code. The magic lies in the `data-` attributes added to the input HTML elements based on the Data Annotation attributes. This jQuery unobtrusive library gets a list of fields for which `data-` attributes are added and it gets validated.

Run the application and press *Ctrl + U* to see the source code. The source code will look something like the following:

```
<div>
    <form method="post" role="form" action="/">
        <table>
            <tr>
                <td><label for="Name">Name</label></td>
                <td><input type="text" data-val="true" data-val-required="Employee Name is required" id="Name" name="Name" value="" /></td>
                <td><span id="validationName" style="color:red" class="field-validation-valid" data-valmsg-for="Name" data-valmsg-replace="true"></span></td>
            </tr>
            <tr>
                <td><label for="Designation">Designation</label></td>
                <td><input type="text" data-val="true" data-val-minlength="Minimum length of designation should be 5 characters" data-val-minlength-min="5" data-val-required="Employee Designation is required" id="Designation" name="Designation" value="" /></td>
                <td><span id="validationDesignation" style="color:red" class="field-validation-valid" data-valmsg-for="Designation" data-valmsg-replace="true"></span></td>
            </tr>
            <tr>
                <td><label for="Salary">Salary</label></td>
                <td><input type="text" data-val="true" data-val-number="The field Salary must be a number " data-val-range="The field Salary must be between 1000 and
9999.99. " data-val-range-max="9999.99" data-val-range-min="1000" data-val-required="The Salary field is required." id="Salary" name="Salary" value="0.00" /></td>
                <td><span id="validationSalary" style="color:red" class="field-validation-valid" data-valmsg-for="Salary" data-valmsg-replace="true"></span></td>
            </tr>
            <tr>
                <td colspan="2"><input type="submit" id="submitbutton" value="Submit" /></td>
            </tr>
        </table>
        <input name="__RequestVerificationToken" type="hidden" value="CfD3S5ynGVnuIo93k-
ZC@mwuRmQIi3Rr2rfOOjOinJqrBbEtTXIptb6p98ZSforN6kfRpp5KaUprON7Mx15ypXrRHgEaf7QIFOJuB2ccKeedHk8?2n6YSA?toB3LCTkAZS5Y1xfT3iLt3FD7HQ-62t5HuV0" /></form>
</div>
```

Different attributes will be added to different kinds of Data Annotation attributes. For the fields to be validated, the `data-val` attribute would be set to `true`. For the properties which are marked as required in the View model, the `data-val-required` attribute will have the value of the error message of the associated property.

Implementation

There will be a layout file (`_Layout.cshtml`) to define the layout structure of your web application. As JavaScript libraries are going to be used in all the pages, this is the right place to add common functionalities such as unobtrusive validation. Just add the JavaScript libraries (highlighted in bold) to the layout file (`_Layout.cshtml`) so that they will be available for all the `View` files:

```
<!DOCTYPE html>
<html>
<head>
    <meta name="viewport" content="width=device-width" />
    <title>@ViewBag.Title</title>
</head>
<body>
    <div>
        @RenderBody()
    </div>

    <script
src="http://ajax.aspnetcdn.com/ajax/jQuery/jquery-2.2.3.js"></script>
    <script
src="https://ajax.aspnetcdn.com/ajax/jquery.validate/1.14.0/jquery.validate
```

```
.min.js"></script>
    <script
src="https://ajax.aspnetcdn.com/ajax/mvc/5.2.3/jquery.validate.unobtrusive.
min.js"></script>
</body>
</html>
```

There is no change to the View model except for the removal of the JavaScript function we wrote earlier for validating the fields. The complete code for the view is as following:

```
@model Validation.ViewModels.EmployeeAddViewModel

<div>

    <form asp-controller="Employee" asp-action="Index" method="post"
role="form">
        <table>
            <tr>
                <td><label asp-for="Name"></label></td>
                <td><input asp-for="Name" /></td>
                <td><span id="validationName" asp-validation-for="Name"
style="color:red"></span></td>
            </tr>
            <tr>
                <td><label asp-for="Designation"></label> </td>
                <td><input asp-for="Designation" /></td>
                <td><span id="validationDesignation" asp-validation-
for="Designation" style="color:red"></span> </td>
            </tr>
            <tr>
                <td><label asp-for="Salary"></label></td>
                <td><input asp-for="Salary"></td>
                <td> <span id="validationSalary" asp-validation-
for="Salary" style="color:red"></span> </td>
            </tr>
            <tr>
                <td colspan="2"><input type="submit" id="submitbutton"
value="Submit" /></td>
            </tr>

        </table>
    </form>

</div>

<br /><br /> <br />

<b> List of employees:</b> <br />
```

```
<div>
    <table border="1">
        <tr>
            <th> ID </th>
            <th> Name </th>
            <th> Designation </th>
            <th> Salary </th>
        </tr>
        @foreach (var employee in Model.EmployeesList)
        {
            <tr>
                <td>@employee.EmployeeId</td>
                <td>@employee.Name</td>
                <td>@employee.Designation</td>
                <td>@employee.Salary</td>
            </tr>
        }
    </table>

</div>
```

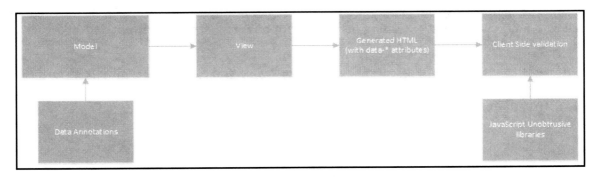

The preceding diagram depicts the unobtrusive client validation process:

1. Data Annotations are added to Model/ViewModels.
2. The view takes Model/ViewModels and generates the HTML.
3. The generated HTML from the View model contains data-* attributes:

   - For the fields for which the Required attribute is set, the data-val-required attribute is created with the error message as its value.
   - For the fields with the MinLength Data Annotation attribute, the data-val-minlength attribute is set with the error message as its value.

- For the range Data Annotation, the `data-val-range` attribute is set with the error message as its value. The `data-val-range-max` represents the maximum value in the range and the `data-val-range-min` attribute represents the minimum value in the range.

4. The jQuery unobtrusive validation library reads these elements with `data-*` attributes and does the client-side validation. This allows the developer to not write the separation validation code using JavaScript as everything is resolved by the configuration itself.

Summary

In this chapter, we have learned about the need for validation and the different kinds of validation available. We have even discussed how client-side and server-side validation work, along with the pros and cons of each type of validation. Later, we made code changes to validate the input data at the server-side. Then we used JavaScript to validate the input data in the client-side itself. Finally, we used the jQuery unobtrusive library to do the client-side validation without ever writing the JavaScript code to validate the input data at the client-side.

In the next chapter, we will discuss the routing principle and how to customize it. In an earlier chapter, we saw the basics of routing in an ASP.NET 5 application. Now we are going to explore the topic in depth.

7
Routing

Routing is one of the important concepts in the ASP.NET MVC application as it takes care of incoming requests and maps them to the appropriate controller's actions.

In this chapter, we are going to learn about the following topics:

- Using the `MapRoute` method to configure routing
- Different types of routing with examples—convention and attribute-based
- Using HTTP verbs in attribute-based routing

We briefly discussed routing in `Chapter 3`, *Controllers*. In this chapter, we are going to discuss routing along with several options available to customize it in ASP.NET Core.

Convention-based routing

The routing engine is responsible for mapping the incoming requests to the appropriate action method of the controller.

In the `Configure` method of the `Startup` class, we have mapped the following route:

```
app.UseMvc(routes =>
    {
        routes.MapRoute(name: "default",
        template: "{controller=Employee}/{action=Index}/{id?}");
    });
```

The `MapRoute` method has two parameters:

- `name`: This represents the name of the route as we could configure multiple routes for the same application.
- `template`: This signifies the actual configuration for the route. There are three parts to this configuration value. As we are supplying default parameters, if the values are not passed, it will take the default parameter values.

- `{controller=Employee}`: The first value acts as the name of the controller and we use the `Employee` controller as the default controller when the controller value is not available in the URL.
- `{action=Index}`: The `Index` action method will be acting as the default action method and the second parameter from the URL will be taken as the action method name.
- `{id?}`: By specifying "?" after the `id` parameter, we are saying that `id` is the optional parameter. If the value is passed as the third parameter, the `id` value will be taken. Otherwise, it would not be considered.

There is another method with the same functionality. The `app.UseMvcWithDefaultRoute()` method configures the route `"{controller=Employee}/{action=Index}/{id?}"`. But we have used the earlier method to show that we can customize the route as we want.

Let us see a few examples and observe how our routing engine works. We are assuming the following routing for the preceding examples:

```
"{controller=Employee}/{action=Index}/{id?}"
```

Example 1

URL-`http://localhost:49831/`

In this URL, we have not passed a value for the `controller`, `action`, or `id`. Since we have not passed anything, it would take the default values for the controller and the action. So, the URL is converted into the following URL by the routing engine:

```
http://localhost:49831/Employee/Index
```

Example 2

URL-`http://localhost:49831/Employee/`

In this URL, we have passed the value for the `controller` (the first parameter), which is `Employee`, whereas we did not pass anything for `action` method (the second parameter) or `id` (the third parameter). So, the URL will be converted into the following URL by taking the default value for the `action` method:

`http://localhost:49831/Employee/Index`

Example 3

URL-`http://localhost:49831/Manager/List`

The routing engine will take the first parameter, `Manager`, as the `controller` method name and the second parameter, `List`, as the `action` method name.

Example 4

URL-`http://localhost:49831/Manager/Details/2`

We have passed all three parameters in this URL. So, the first parameter value, `Manager`, will be considered as the `controller` method name, the second parameter value will be considered as the `action` method name, and the third parameter value will be considered as the `id` method name.

When defining the map route, we have used the `MapRoute` method with a couple of parameters. The first parameter, `name`, represents the name of the route and the second parameter, `template`, represents the URL pattern to be matched along with the default values:

```
routes.MapRoute(name: "default",
            template: "{controller=Employee}/{action=Index}/{id?}");
```

There are other overloaded variations of this `MapRoute` method. The following is another commonly overloaded `MapRoute` method, where the incoming URL pattern and the default values are passed for different parameters. The name of the route is `FirstRoute` and this route will be applied for all URLs starting with `Home`. The default values for the controller and the action are `Home` and `Index2` respectively:

```
routes.MapRoute(name:"FirstRoute",
                template:"Home",
                defaults:new {controller ="Home", action="Index2"});
```

You can define any number of routing maps for your ASP.NET MVC application. There is no restriction or limit on the routing maps. Let us add another routing map to our application. We have added another route map called `FirstRoute` to our application (highlighted in bold):

```
public void Configure(IApplicationBuilder app)
    {
        app.UseIISPlatformHandler();
        app.UseMvc(routes =>
        {
            routes.MapRoute(name:"FirstRoute",
            template:"Home", defaults:new {controller ="Home",
action="Index2"});

            routes.MapRoute(name: "default",
            template: "{controller=Employee}/{action=Index}/{id?}");
        });
    }
```

And we have added another `controller` method by the name `HomeController` with a couple of simple `action` methods returning different strings:

```
public class HomeController : Controller
    {
        // GET: /<controller>/
        public IActionResult Index()
        {
            return Content("Index action method");
        }

        public IActionResult Index2()
        {
            return Content("Index2 action method");
        }
    }
```

When you try to access the application through the URL,
`http://localhost:49831/Hello`, both routing maps, `FirstRoute` and the `default`,
match with the URL pattern.

Which map routing, do you think, will get applied in this scenario?

The routing engine maps the incoming URL based on the following factors:

1. Matching pattern.
2. On the order defined in the routing engine.

The first factor is an obvious one. For a routing map to be picked up by the routing engine,
the pattern of the incoming URL should get matched with the defined template in the
routing map.

The second factor is subtle but important. If more than one routing map matches with the
incoming URL, the routing engine will pick the first URL as defined in the configuration.
For example, if the incoming URL matches with both the `FirstRoute` and `default` maps,
the routing engine will pick the `FirstRoute` map as it was defined first in the
configuration.

If the routing engine could not map the incoming URL to any of the mapping routes, we get an `HTTP 404 error`, meaning that no resource could be found. You can see the status (200 means *OK*, 404 means *No resource found*) by looking at the **Network** tab in the developer tools as shown in the following screenshot:

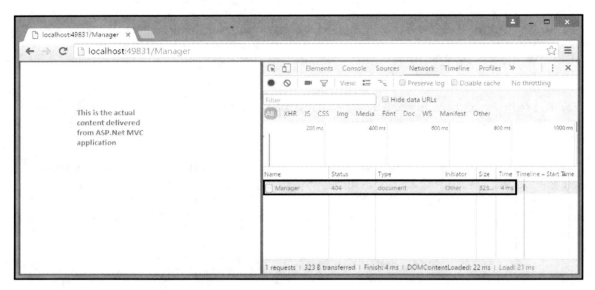

Attribute-based routing

Until now, we have used convention-based routing. In convention-based routing, we define the routing templates (which are just parameterized strings) in a centralized place these are applicable to all the available controllers. The problem with convention-based routing is that, if we want to define different URL patterns for different controllers, we need to define a custom URL pattern that is common to all the controllers. This makes things difficult.

There is another option for configuring the routing engine-attribute-based routing. In attribute-based routing, instead of configuring all the routing in a centralized location, the configuration will happen at the controller level.

Let us see an example of attribute-based routing.

First, let us remove the convention-based routing that we created earlier in the `Configure` method in the `startup.cs` class file:

```
public void Configure(IApplicationBuilder app)
    {
        app.UseIISPlatformHandler();
        app.UseMvc();
        //app.UseMvc(routes =>
        //{
        //      routes.MapRoute(name: "FirstRoute",
        //                      template: "Hello",
        //                      defaults: new { controller = "Home",
        //                      action = "Index2" });

        //      routes.MapRoute(name: "default",
        //                template:"
        //                {controller=Employee}/{action=Index}/{id?}");
        //});
    }
```

Then, we can configure the routing at the controller itself. In the following code, we have added the routing configuration for the home controller that we created earlier:

```
namespace Validation.Controllers
{
    public class HomeController : Controller
    {
        // GET: /<controller>/
        [Route("Home")]
        public IActionResult Index()
        {
            return Content("Index action method");
        }
        [Route("Home/Index3")]
        public IActionResult Index2()
        {
            return Content("Index2 action method");
        }
    }
}
```

We have used the `Route` attribute in the `action` methods of the controller. The value passed in the `Route` attribute will be acting as the URL pattern. For example, when we access the URL `http://localhost:49831/Home/`, the `Index` method of `HomeController` will be called. When we access the URL `http://localhost:49831/Home/Index3`, the `Index2` method of `HomeController` will be called. Please note that the URL pattern and `action` method name do not need to match. In the preceding example, we are calling the `Index2` action method but the URL pattern uses `Index3`, `http://localhost:49831/Home/Index3`.

When you use attribute-based routing and convention-based routing together, attribute-based routing will take precedence.

Route attribute at the controller level

You will notice that, with the URL pattern for the `action` methods, `Index` and `Index2`, we repeat the controller name, `Home`, in both URL patterns, `Home` and `Home/Index3`. Instead of repeating the `controller` method name (or any common part in the URL) at the `action` method level, we can define it at the `controller` level.

In the following code, the common part of the URL (`Home`) is defined at the `controller` level and the unique part is defined at the `action` method level. When the URL pattern is getting mapped to the `action` methods of the controller, both route parts (at the `controller` level and at the `action` method level) are merged and matched. So there will be no difference between the routes defined earlier and those that follow.

If you want two parameters in attribute-based routing, you can pass them within curly braces. In the following example, we did this for the `SayHello` action method.

For example, the URL pattern `http://localhost:49831/Home/Index3`, will still get mapped to `Index2` method of the `Homecontroller`:

```
namespace Validation.Controllers
{
    [Route("Home")]
    public class HomeController : Controller
    {
        // GET: /<controller>/
        [Route("")]
        public IActionResult Index()
        {
            return Content("Index action method");
        }
```

```
[Route("Index3")]
public IActionResult Index2()
{
    return Content("Index2 action method");
}

[Route("SayHello/{id}")]
public IActionResult SayHello(int id)
{
    return Content("Say Hello action method"+id);
}
    }
}
```

Passing routing values in HTTP action verbs in the Controller

Instead of passing the routing values as `Route` attributes, we can even pass the routing values in HTTP action verbs such as `HTTPGet` and `HTTPPost`.

In the following code, we have used the `HTTPGet` attribute to pass the route values. For the `Index` method, we did not pass any value and hence no route value will get appended to the route value defined at the `controller` method level. For the `Index2` method, we are passing the value `Index3` and `Index3` will get appended to the route value defined at the `controller` level. Please note that only URLs with `GET` methods will be mapped to the `action` methods. If you access the same URL pattern with the `POST` method, these routes will not get matched and hence these `action` methods will not get called.

```
namespace Validation.Controllers
{
    [Route("Home")]
    public class HomeController : Controller
    {
        // GET: /<controller>/
        [HttpGet()]
        public IActionResult Index()
        {
            return Content("Index action method");
        }

        [HttpGet("Index3")]
        public IActionResult Index2()
        {
```

```
            return Content("Index2 action method");
        }
    }
}
```

Route Constraints

Route Constraints enable you to constrain the type of values that you pass to the controller action. For example, if you want to restrict the value to be passed to the int type int, you can do so. The following is one such instance:

```
[HttpGet("details/{id:int?}")]
    public IActionResult Details(int id)
    {
        return View();
    }
```

ASP.NET 5 (ASP.NET Core) even supports default parameter values so that you can pass the default parameters:

```
[HttpGet("details/{id:int = 123}")]
    public IActionResult Details(int id)
    {
        return View();
    }
```

Summary

In this chapter, we have learned about routing and how it works. We learned about different kinds of routing available. We discussed convention-based routing and attribute-based routing with different examples. We also discussed route constraints and the default parameter values that could be passed.

In the next chapter, we are going to see how we can make the application look good.

8

Beautifying ASP.NET MVC Applications with Bootstrap

You might have created an application with all the required functionalities. It may even work perfectly without any issues in all scenarios. But the success of your application depends on how well your users can access it. Your application should look good (if not great) and be user-friendly in order for it to be a success.

In this chapter, you are going to learn about the following topics:

- Role of HTML and CSS in the ASP.NET Core application
- Characteristics of front-end frameworks and different frameworks available
- Bootstrap and its grid system along its features
- CSS classes available in Bootstrap for form elements such as input and select elements
- CSS classes for different types of HTML elements such as table
- Using Bootstrap in your ASP.NET Core application

Before discussing how to make our application look good, let us take a step back and discuss the roles that HTML and CSS play in your application.

Knowing HTML and CSS

As mentioned earlier, all browsers can only understand HTML, CSS, and JavaScript. So, the applications that you build should produce output as HTML, CSS, and JavaScript. This holds true for web applications built using other technologies such as Java or Ruby on Rails. Having said that, we will only discuss HTML and CSS.

HTML (Hyper Text Markup Language) is used to structure the content in your web pages. For example, you can add content in a `title` tag so that it will be available in a browser's tab or window. Let us see an example.

Open any text editor (you can even use Notepad), type the following HTML content and the save file as `Bootstrap.html`. Please note the extension `.html`:

```
<!DOCTYPE html>
<html>
<head>
    <title> Beautify your ASP.NET MVC applications using Bootstrap </title>
</head>
<body>
    <h1> Bootstrap </h1>
    <p>
        Bootstrap is the most popular HTML, CSS, and JS framework for
developing responsive, mobile first projects on the web.
    </p>
</body>
</html>
```

The first line tells that the HTML content follows HTML 5 standards (the latest and the current version of HTML) and should be interpreted as such. The `html` tag tells the browser it is the start of an HTML document. Information in the `head` tag represents metadata and tells the browser to the web page rather than the web page itself. Examples include the page title, description about the page, and keywords for the search engine optimization. All the contents of the `body` tag will be shown in the browser's main window. In the preceding HTML code, we have made `Bootstrap` the heading and the rest of the content has been made as a paragraph.

Open the file in the browser and you should see something like the following screenshot:

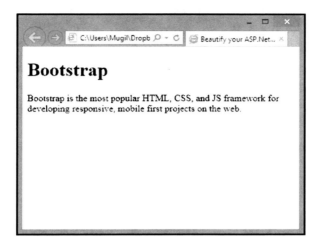

You will notice the content placed in the `title` tag shown as the browser's tab title, the heading content is made bold and bigger in size, and the paragraph starts on a new line.

CSS is all about styling. You can use CSS to customize how each of the elements in your web page looks. You can change the color of the button, the font of the heading text, the border size of a table, and so on. You can include CSS styles either inline or using a separate file. If you are using inline CSS, it should be within a `style` tag. If you are using external CSS, we can make use of a `link` tag and refer to the external CSS file.

CSS is nothing but a set of rules used for the presentation. Each rule consists of two parts—a selector for which a declaration has to be applied and a declaration containing the styling information. The styling information has a property and a value for the property.

Let us take the following simple CSS rule:

```
h1{
     color : #0094ff;
}
```

This CSS rule states that all the heading text should be in a blue color. `h1` is the selector, which tells the browser the following declaration has to be applied for all `h1` tags. In the declaration, we are setting the blue color (`#0094ff` is blue in hexadecimal format).

The following is the updated HTML file where I've updated the CSS styles (highlighted in bold):

```
<!DOCTYPE html>
<html>
<head>
    <title> Beautify your ASP.NET MVC applications using Bootstrap </title>
    <style type="text/css">
        body{
            font-family:Arial,Verdana,sans-serif;
        }

        h1{
            color : #0094ff;
        }

        p {
            color: #5f5e5e;
        }
    </style>

</head>
<body>
    <h1> Bootstrap </h1>
    <p>
        Bootstrap is the most popular HTML, CSS, and JS framework for
developing responsive, mobile first projects on the web.
    </p>
</body>
</html>
```

When you open the file in a browser after making the style changes, you will get the following output:

Having said that, you need to create CSS rules to make the elements in your web application look good. But creating different styles for each element is a time-consuming and tedious task. You can choose from any of the frontend frameworks available.

Any application should have the following characteristics:

- **Consistency**: The elements and the controls that are being used by your application should be familiar to the user. For example, if you use a drop-down list, the user should be able to select only one value from it.
- **Responsive**: The application that you build should look good across all devices of different sizes. The code that you write should adapt to the screen size of the device of your users.
- **Mobile-friendly**: This is related to the preceding point. These days, many applications being accessed from mobile devices rather than desktops or laptops. We have to make sure that the application that we build will look great on mobile devices.
- **Customizable**: If you are going to use any front-end application framework, it should be customizable according to your needs. For example, if you want to update the heading text color, you should be able to update or override the CSS file to make the necessary changes.
- **Easy to get started**: The learning curve for learning your front-end framework should be minimal as you should be spending time on delivering value to the customer—building and delivering the solution. We are not getting paid to learn a new fancy front-end framework.

There are few front-end frameworks available such as Bootstrap, **Foundation**, and **PureCSS**. In this chapter, we are going to use the Bootstrap framework as it is the most widely used front-end framework.

Bootstrap

Bootstrap is the most popular HTML, CSS, and JS framework for developing responsive, mobile-first projects on the web and you can access it at `http://getbootstrap.com/`.

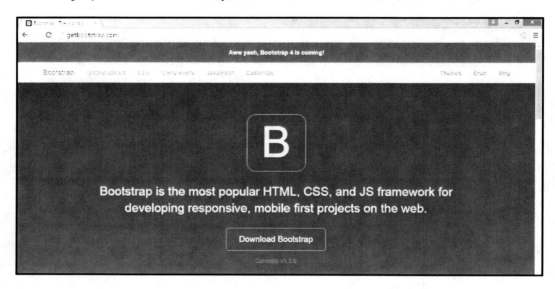

Bootstrap has many features that meet the various needs of a web application. It has different CSS classes for each of the HTML elements so that you can use it without touching any CSS code. However, if you wish to override it, you can do so.

Let us look at each of the features of Bootstrap in brief.

Bootstrap Grid system

The grid system in Bootstrap helps you to create a responsive layout for your application. This feature makes your application look great in all devices of different shapes including mobile devices.

Bootstrap provides a fluid grid system, which scales up to twelve columns as the device or viewport size increases. You can think of grid system as being like columns in an Excel sheet (like the one in the following screenshot):

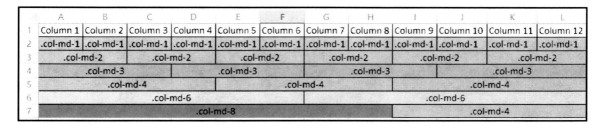

We can combine multiple columns to create a wider column. In the second row in the preceding screenshot, we have used a single column (using class .col-md-1) twelve times. In the third row, we are using a CSS class (.col-md-2) to create six wider columns instead of twelve shorter columns. Likewise, we are creating a lesser number of wider columns.

Forms

All form controls receive global styling when you use Bootstrap in your application. The following is one such example (the screenshot is taken from the Bootstrap site):

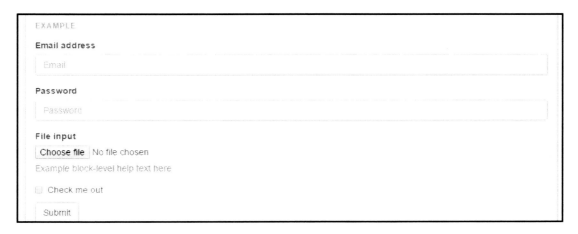

The following is the code for the preceding form. Related HTML elements are grouped together in the form. For example, the labels for the Email and **Email address** input text boxes are grouped together. The same is the case for **Password** and **File input**.

```html
<form>
  <div class="form-group">
    <label for="exampleInputEmail1">Email address</label>
    <input type="email" class="form-control" id="exampleInputEmail1" placeholder="Email">
  </div>
  <div class="form-group">
    <label for="exampleInputPassword1">Password</label>
    <input type="password" class="form-control" id="exampleInputPassword1" placeholder="Password">
  </div>
  <div class="form-group">
    <label for="exampleInputFile">File input</label>
    <input type="file" id="exampleInputFile">
    <p class="help-block">Example block-level help text here.</p>
  </div>
  <div class="checkbox">
    <label>
      <input type="checkbox"> Check me out
    </label>
  </div>
  <button type="submit" class="btn btn-default">Submit</button>
</form>
```

Inline forms

Inline forms are forms where all the form elements are on the same line (as shown in the following screenshot). We need to add the class `form-inline` to the `form` element.

```html
<form class="form-inline">
  <div class="form-group">
    <label for="exampleInputName2">Name</label>
    <input type="text" class="form-control" id="exampleInputName2" placeholder="Jane Doe">
  </div>
  <div class="form-group">
    <label for="exampleInputEmail2">Email</label>
    <input type="email" class="form-control" id="exampleInputEmail2" placeholder="jane.doe@example.com">
  </div>
  <button type="submit" class="btn btn-default">Send invitation</button>
</form>
```

Horizontal forms

In horizontal forms, we have each element group on a separate line; **Email** label, Email input on a line and **Password** label, Password input on a line (as shown in the following screenshot):

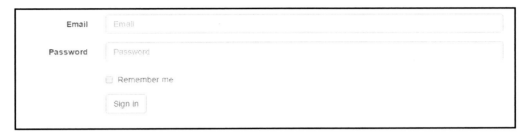

To apply the horizontal form styling, we just need to add the class `form-horizontal` as in the following code. Just like other forms, we need to group the related HTML elements together by applying the CSS class `form-group`:

```html
<form class="form-horizontal">
  <div class="form-group">
    <label for="inputEmail3" class="col-sm-2 control-label">Email</label>
    <div class="col-sm-10">
      <input type="email" class="form-control" id="inputEmail3" placeholder="Email">
    </div>
  </div>
  <div class="form-group">
    <label for="inputPassword3" class="col-sm-2 control-label">Password</label>
    <div class="col-sm-10">
      <input type="password" class="form-control" id="inputPassword3" placeholder="Password">
    </div>
  </div>
  <div class="form-group">
    <div class="col-sm-offset-2 col-sm-10">
      <div class="checkbox">
        <label>
          <input type="checkbox"> Remember me
        </label>
      </div>
    </div>
  </div>
  <div class="form-group">
    <div class="col-sm-offset-2 col-sm-10">
      <button type="submit" class="btn btn-default">Sign in</button>
    </div>
  </div>
</form>
```

Table CSS classes

For basic styling, add the base CSS class `table` to the `table` HTML element as shown in the following screenshot:

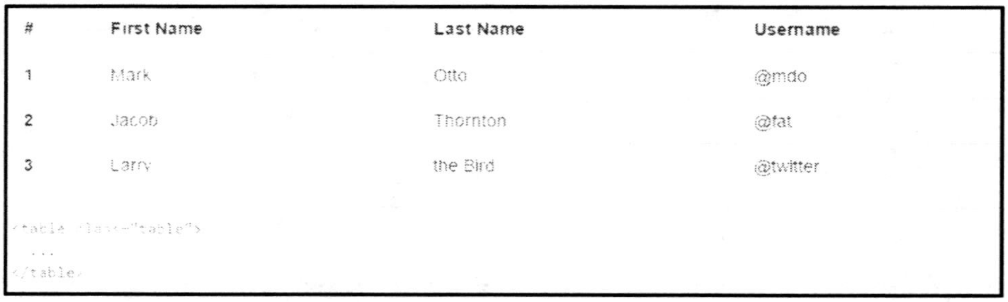

#	First Name	Last Name	Username
1	Mark	Otto	@mdo
2	Jacob	Thornton	@fat
3	Larry	the Bird	@twitter

```
<table class="table">
...
</table>
```

Striped tables

In a striped table, the background of alternate rows will be of the same color. In the following screenshot, the background color of the first row and third row are the same color. You can apply the `table-striped` class to apply the striped table behavior to the table HTML element.

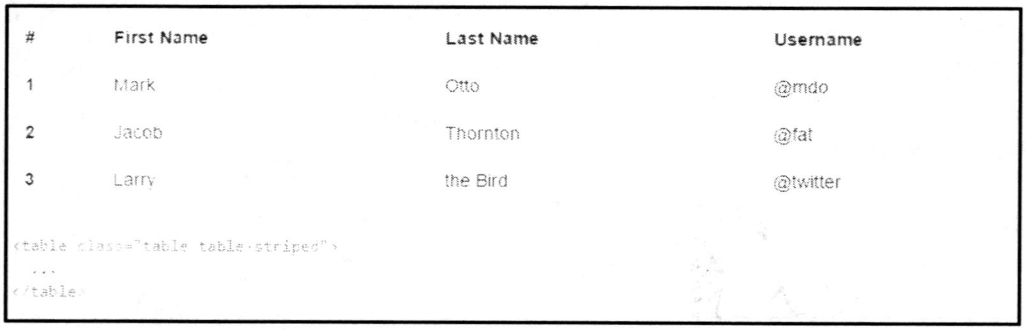

#	First Name	Last Name	Username
1	Mark	Otto	@mdo
2	Jacob	Thornton	@fat
3	Larry	the Bird	@twitter

```
<table class="table table-striped">
...
</table>
```

Hover tables

When you move your mouse over any of the rows in the table, the background color of the row is changed. This hover behavior can be achieved by applying the CSS class `table-hover` along with the class `table` to the HTML table element.

#	First Name	Last Name	Username
1	Mark	Otto	@mdo
2	Jacob	Thornton	@fat
3	Larry	the Bird	@twitter

```
<table class="table table-hover">
    ...
</table>
```

Bordered tables

We can have a bordered table (as in the following screenshot), if we apply the CSS class `table-bordered` to the `table` element.

#	First Name	Last Name	Username
1	Mark	Otto	@mdo
2	Jacob	Thornton	@fat
3	Larry	the Bird	@twitter

```
<table class="table table-bordered">
    ...
</table>
```

Contextual classes in table

There are times when you want to highlight rows based on the data value. For example, if you are showing inventory data in tabular format, you might want to highlight the rows with a red background color for the items whose count is less than the stipulated count. In this case, you can apply a `danger` class to table rows to highlight them in a red color. There are different types of contextual class available for highlighting in different colors. You can apply these classes to individual cells instead of the complete rows.

Contextual classes

Use contextual classes to color table rows or individual cells.

Class	Description
.active	Applies the hover color to a particular row or cell
.success	Indicates a successful or positive action
.info	Indicates a neutral informative change or action
.warning	Indicates a warning that might need attention
.danger	Indicates a dangerous or potentially negative action

EXAMPLE

#	Column heading	Column heading	Column heading
1	Column content	Column content	Column content
2	Column content	Column content	Column content
3	Column content	Column content	Column content
4	Column content	Column content	Column content
5	Column content	Column content	Column content
6	Column content	Column content	Column content
7	Column content	Column content	Column content
8	Column content	Column content	Column content

Buttons

There are different styling options available for making buttons appear in different colors. For all the buttons, the base button class `btn` has to be applied:

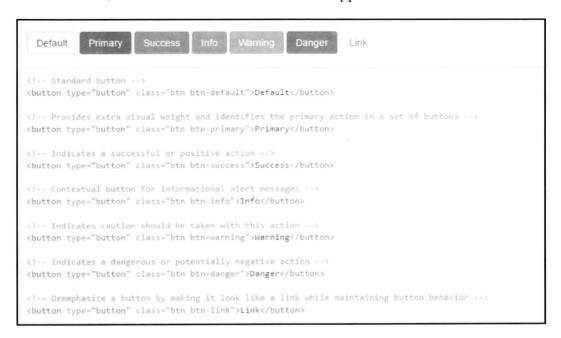

The `btn-primary` button class is used to highlight the button in blue whereas the `btn-success` button class highlights the button in green. In the preceding screenshot, different options for styling the button are shown.

Button sizes

You can change the size of the button according to your needs. The `btn-lg` class can be applied to a large button and the `btn-sm` class can be applied to buttons to make them appear small. The following are the different options available to control the size of the button.

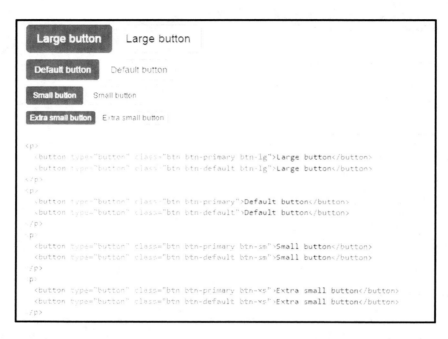

Contextual colors

Based on the context, you might want to change the color of the text. For example, you might want to make the text appear in green if the previous operation is successful. For an unsuccessful operation, you might want to show the error message in a red. In such scenarios, you might use this helper CSS classes to show them in different colors.

```
Fusce dapibus, tellus ac cursus commodo, tortor mauris nibh.

Nullam id dolor id nibh ultricies vehicula ut id elit.

Duis mollis, est non commodo luctus, nisi erat porttitor ligula.

Maecenas sed diam eget risus varius blandit sit amet non magna.

Etiam porta sem malesuada magna mollis euismod.

Donec ullamcorper nulla non metus auctor fringilla.


<p class="text-muted">...</p>
<p class="text-primary">...</p>
<p class="text-success">...</p>
<p class="text-info">...</p>
<p class="text-warning">...</p>
<p class="text-danger">...</p>
```

We have seen various features of Bootstrap. Now, let us use Bootstrap to make our application look good. Basically, we have two major components in our view—a form at the top to get the input from the user and a table at the bottom to display the results in a table.

Using Bootstrap in your ASP.NET MVC application

There are different ways to get Bootstrap for your application:

- Refer to the Bootstrap file available at the CDN (Content Delivery Network) in your application
- Download the source code
- Install with Bower
- Compile with Grunt

Of these options, the easiest option is the first one.

Open the layout file (`_Layout.cshtml`) in the application that we created earlier. Include the CSS files at the top (within the `head` tag) and the scripts at the bottom (at the end of the `body` tag):

```
<!DOCTYPE html>

<html>
<head>
    <meta name="viewport" content="width=device-width" />
    <title>@ViewBag.Title</title>
```

```html
    <!-- Latest compiled and minified CSS -->
    <link rel="stylesheet"
href="https://maxcdn.bootstrapcdn.com/bootstrap/3.3.6/css/bootstrap.min.css
"
    integrity="sha384-1q8mTJOASx8j1Au+a5WDVnPi2lkFfwwEAa8hDDdjZlpLegxhjVME1fgjW
PGmkzs7" crossorigin="anonymous">
    <!-- Optional theme -->
    <link rel="stylesheet"
href="https://maxcdn.bootstrapcdn.com/bootstrap/3.3.6/css/bootstrap-theme.m
in.css" integrity="sha384-
fLW2N01lMqjakBkx3l/M9EahuwpSfeNvV63J5ezn3uZzapT0u7EYsXMjQV+0En5r"
crossorigin="anonymous">

</head>
<body>
    <div>
        @RenderBody()
    </div>
    <script
src="http://ajax.aspnetcdn.com/ajax/jQuery/jquery-2.2.3.js"></script>
    <script
src="https://ajax.aspnetcdn.com/ajax/jquery.validate/1.14.0/jquery.validate
.min.js"></script>
    <script
src="https://ajax.aspnetcdn.com/ajax/mvc/5.2.3/jquery.validate.unobtrusive.
min.js"></script>
    <!-- Latest compiled and minified JavaScript -->
    <script
src="https://maxcdn.bootstrapcdn.com/bootstrap/3.3.6/js/bootstrap.min.js"
integrity="sha384-0mSbJDEHialfmuBBQP6A4Qrprq5OVfW37PRR3j5ELqxss1yVqOtnepnHV
P9aJ7xS" crossorigin="anonymous"></script>
</body>
</html>
```

Installing with Bower

Right click on the **Project** menu and select the **Manage Bower Packages** option from the **context** menu:

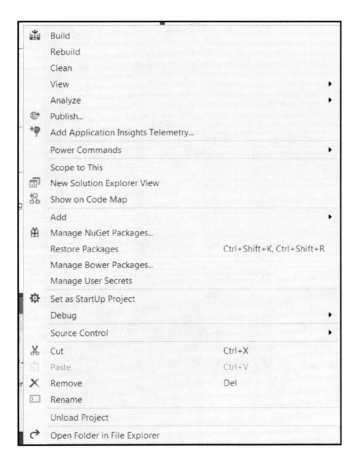

Once you select **Manage Bower Packages,** you will be able to install or uninstall the Bower package just as you installed or uninstalled the NuGet package.

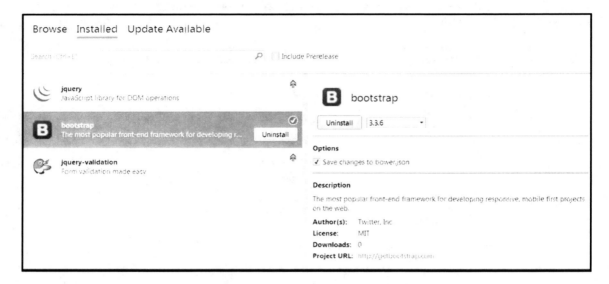

HTML doctype

Bootstrap makes use of certain HTML elements and CSS properties that require the use of HTML 5 doctype. By default, the view that you create in ASP.NET Core will have HTML 5 doctype only. So, we do not need to do anything regarding this.

```
<!DOCTYPE html>

<html lang="en">
...
</html>
```

Let us make the following changes to our screen to make use of Bootstrap:

- Apply the CSS class form-horizontal to the form.
- For the label, input, and validation error spans use the CSS col-sm-2, col-sm-4, and col-sm-3 classes respectively
- For labels, apply the CSS class control-label
- For input HTML elements, the form-control CSS class is applied

- For each of the form groups (containing the HTML elements such as label and input), apply the CSS class `form-group`
- For all validation error messages, apply the `text-danger` CSS class so that they will be shown in red
- Apply the `table`, `table-bordered` CSS class to style the table

The following is the complete updated view code; we have used Bootstrap CSS classes to make our application look great:

```
@model Validation.ViewModels.EmployeeAddViewModel

<div>
    <br/>
    <br/>
    <form asp-controller="Employee" asp-action="Index" method="post"
role="form" class="form-horizontal">
        <div class="form-group">
            <label asp-for="Name" class="col-sm-2 control-label"></label>
            <div class="col-sm-4">
                <input asp-for="Name" class="form-control" />
            </div>
            <div class="col-sm-3 text-danger">
                <span id="validationName" asp-validation-for="Name"
></span>
            </div>
        </div>

        <div class="form-group">
            <label asp-for="Designation" class="col-sm-2 control-
label"></label>
            <div class="col-sm-4">
                <input asp-for="Designation" class="form-control" />
            </div>
            <div class="col-sm-3 text-danger">
                <span id="validationDesignation" asp-validation-
for="Designation" ></span>
            </div>
        </div>

        <div class="form-group">
            <label asp-for="Salary" class="col-sm-2 control-label"></label>
            <div class="col-sm-4">
                <input asp-for="Salary" class="form-control" />
            </div>
            <div class="col-sm-3 text-danger">
```

```html
                    <span id="validationSalary" asp-validation-for="Salary"
></span>
            </div>
        </div>

        <div class="form-group">
            <div class="col-sm-offset-2 col-sm-10">
                <button type="submit" class="btn btn-
primary">Submit</button>
            </div>
        </div>

    </form>
</div>

<br /><br /> <br />

<h4> List of employees:</h4> <br />

    <table class="table table-bordered">
        <tr>
            <th> ID </th>
            <th> Name </th>
            <th> Designation </th>
            <th> Salary </th>
        </tr>
        @foreach (var employee in Model.EmployeesList)
        {
        <tr>
            <td>@employee.EmployeeId</td>
            <td>@employee.Name</td>
            <td>@employee.Designation</td>
            <td>@employee.Salary</td>
        </tr>
        }
    </table>
```

After making the preceding changes, when you run the application, your screen should look something like the following:

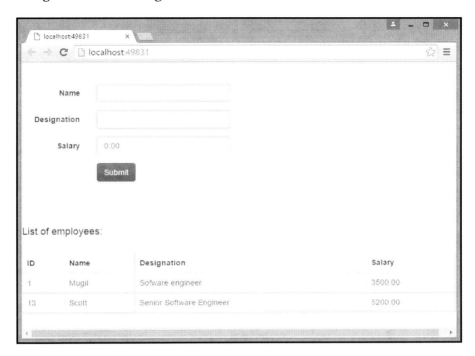

Summary

In this chapter, we have learned about the role of HTML and CSS in any web application including the ASP.NET Core application. We have analyzed the needs of a frontend framework and discussed the features of Bootstrap—the most popular HTML, CSS, and JS framework for developing responsive, mobile-first projects on the web. We have discussed CSS and components available in Bootstrap for different types of HTML elements with examples. Finally, we have discussed how to incorporate Bootstrap in our ASP.NET Core application.

9

Deployment of ASP.NET Core Application

Once we have completed the development for our ASP.NET core application, we need to deploy the application so that it can be accessed by our users.

In any application, irrespective of whether it is the web, desktop, or mobile application, not all the functionalities have been achieved through code. In fact, you should not try to achieve everything through code.

In this chapter, you are going to learn about the following topics:

- Configuration in the ASP.NET Core application
- Signing up to the Microsoft Azure platform
- Deploying the ASP.NET Core application to the Azure Cloud platform

If you have built a web application using any of the previous versions of ASP.NET MVC, there will be a file by the name of `Web.config` (an XML file) where you can configure all the dependencies for your application. But in ASP.NET Core, there will be no `Web.config` file in your solution:

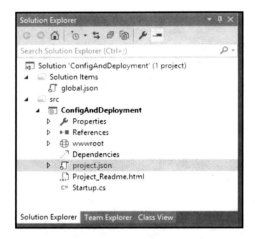

Instead, we have `project.json` (a JSON file), where we will configure the dependencies for your application. Before discussing the contents of `project.json`, let us discuss a bit about JSON.

JSON is an acronym of **JavaScript Object Notation**. It is the open standard data exchange format. It will be in human-readable text and consist of attribute/value pairs. Consider the following JSON, and let's dissect it to see what it represents:

```
{
   "addressess": [
     {
       "DoorNo": 16,
       "Street": "King Street",
       "areaname": "Mascot"
     },
     {
       "DoorNo": 12,
       "Street": "High Street",
       "areaname": "North Sydney"
     }
   ]
}
```

Each piece of data is an attribute value pair, separated by a colon. For example, `"DoorNo"`: `16` tells that the value for `DoorNo` variable is 16 in the first record. Each attribute value pair (sometimes called a property) is separated by a comma. For example, consider the following three properties:

```
"DoorNo": 16,
"Street": "King Street",
"areaname": "Mascot"
```

Each record or object is contained within a pair of curly braces. For example, the following JSON data represents a record or an object:

```
{
    "DoorNo": 16,
    "Street": "King Street",
    "areaname": "Mascot"
}
```

Similar records can be grouped together and could be formed as an array (of objects). Square brackets are used to represent the array in JSON format as in the following example:

```
"addressess": [
  {
    "DoorNo": 16,
    "Street": "King Street",
    "areaname": "Mascot"
  },
  {
    "DoorNo": 12,
    "Street": "High Street",
        "areaname": "North Sydney"
  }
]
```

If we have to represent the same data in XML format, you can do so as follows. Please note that for each piece of information, we should have a start tag and an end tag (ends with "/"):

```
<addresses>
  <address>
    <DoorNo>16</DoorNo>
    <Street>King Street</Street>
    <areaname>Mascot</areaname>
  </address>

  <address>
    <DoorNo>12</DoorNo>
```

```
      <Street>High Street</Street>
      <areaname>North Sydney</areaname>
   </address>
</addresses>
```

The project.json file

All of the project configuration should go into the `project.json` file for the ASP.NET Core application. The following is the `project.json` file that was created when using the predefined ASP.NET Core web application template:

```
{
    "userSecretsId": "aspnet-AzureDeployment-66c8f80c-8186-4ac5-b4c4-9bb79b3f19ef",

    "dependencies": [...],

    "tools": [...],

    "frameworks": [...],

    "buildOptions": [...],

    "runtimeOptions": [...],

    "publishOptions": [...],

    "scripts": [...]
}
```

There are different predefined nodes in this JSON file for different functionalities. Let us take some important nodes in this `project.json` file and discuss them.

The dependencies node

The `dependencies` node lists all the dependencies for your ASP.NET Core application.

The following is a fragment of the `dependencies` node in the ASP.NET Core application. Each dependency is an attribute value pair where the attribute represents the dependency and the value represents the version of the dependency. If you need to provide more information for the dependency, you can have a nested JSON configuration as it is in `Microsoft.NETCore.App`:

```
"dependencies":{
  "Microsoft.NETCore.App":{
    "version": "1.0.0-rc2-3002702",
```

```
"type": "platform"
},
"Microsoft.ApplicationInsights.AspNetCore": "1.0.0-rc2-final",
"Microsoft.AspNetCore.Authentication.Cookies": "1.0.0-rc2- final",
```

The frameworks node

In this node, we mention the frameworks that we depend on for the ASP.NET Core application. `dotnet5.6` represents the full blown .NET framework and `dnxcore50` represents the .NET Core framework containing the subset of functionalities of the complete .NET framework:

```
"frameworks":{
  "netcoreapp1.0":{
    "imports":[
      "dotnet5.6",
      "dnxcore50",
      "portable-net45+win8"
      ]
    }
  },
```

Microsoft Azure

Microsoft Azure is a cloud computing platform and infrastructure from Microsoft for building, deploying, and managing applications and services. It supports different programming languages and arrays of services.

You can deploy your application in any server with **Internet Information Service (IIS)** in your network. But this restricts your application to being accessed only from within your network, assuming your server could only be accessed from within your network (as in most network setups). In this section, we are going to deploy the ASP.NET Core application in Microsoft Azure so that your users across the globe can access your application.

Signing up to Microsoft Azure

In order for your application to be deployed to Azure, you need to have an account with Azure. You can create an Azure account for free and you'll have sufficient credits to deploy your application for free within the first 30 days (`https://azure.microsoft.com/en-in/`):

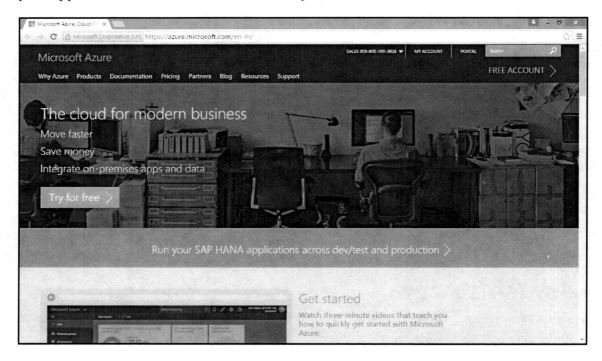

Click the **Try for free** button or **Free Account** link in the top right-hand corner and you'll be forwarded to the following page:

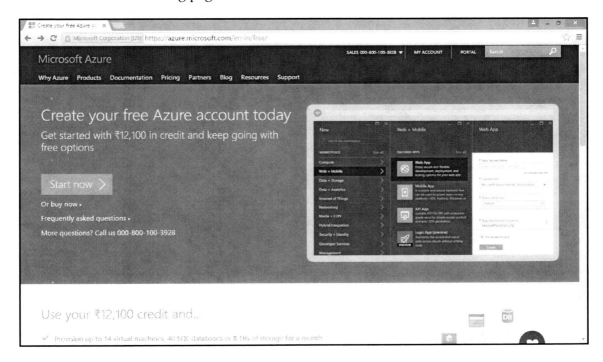

Click the **Start now** button and you'll be redirected to the following page. Enter your Microsoft account credentials and click the **Sign In** button. If you don't have a Microsoft account, you can create one by clicking on the **sign up now** link at the bottom of the page:

As I have a Microsoft account already, I have signed in with my credentials. Once you have signed-in, you will be asked for details about your country, first name, second name, and your work phone, as follows:

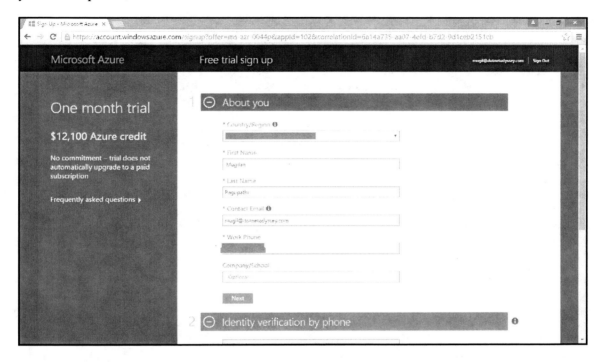

Once you have entered all the necessary details, you will be asked for your country code and phone number so that Azure can text you or call you to verify you are a real person and not a robot 🙂. If you choose the option of **text me**, you will get a code to your mobile phone; you need to enter it in the last field and click **Verify Code**:

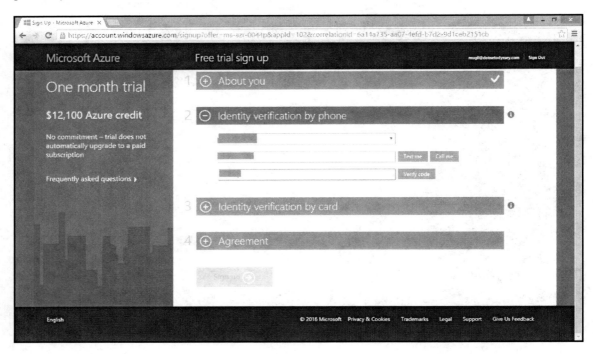

Once you have been verified by phone, you need to enter your credit card information in the following form. You'll be billed for approximately $1 and it will be refunded within five to six business days back to your account. This information is collected to identify the user's identity and the user will not be billed unless the user explicitly opted for the paid service:

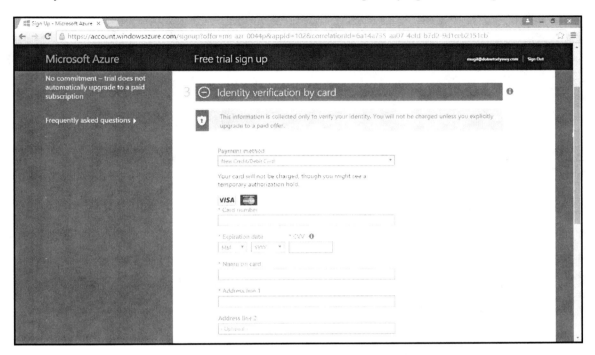

Once you enter your credit card information and click **Next,** you will have to agree to the subscription agreement as the final step in the sign-up process:

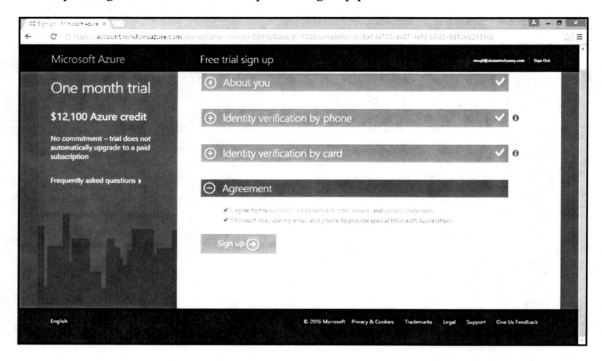

Once you click the **Sign up** button, it will take another five minutes to complete the process. You'll be shown the following screen until the process completes:

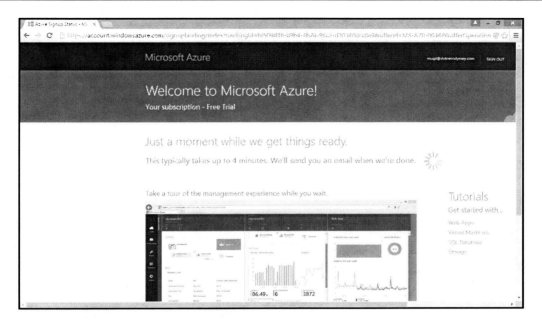

Once the sign-up process completes, you'll be shown the following screen. You'll also get a confirmation e-mail (to the e-mail ID that you gave in the first step) with the subscription details:

Prerequisites to Azure deployment

In order to publish the ASP.NET Core application to Azure from the Visual Studio 2015 Community Edition, you should have Visual Studio 2015 Update 2 installed (at least) and you should install/enable the SQL Server Data Tools.

If you have the latest version of VS 2015, there is no need to install Update 2.

You can download the Visual Studio 2015 Update 2 from the URL at `https://www.visuals tudio.com/en-us/news/vs2015-update2-vs.aspx` and install it.

To install the SQL Server Data Tools, go to **Control Panel | Programs and Features**. Right-click on the **Microsoft Visual Studio Community 2015** and select the **Change**, option, as shown in the following screenshot:

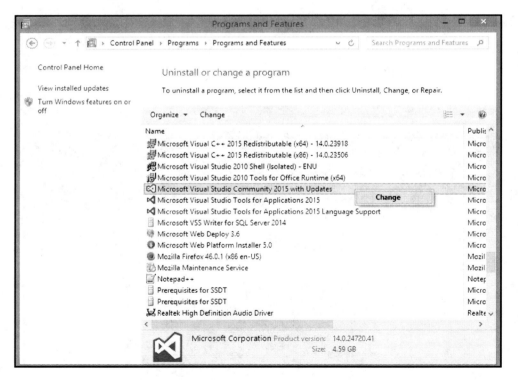

Once you click on **Change** option, you will get the following window—where you have to choose the **Modify** button. Once you click the **Modify** button, you'll be given an option where you can modify the Visual Studio installation options. I have selected **Microsoft SQL Server Data Tools** , as depicted in the following screenshot:

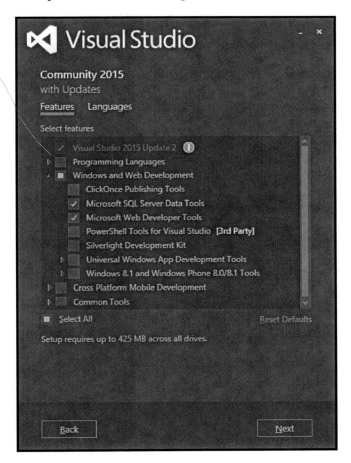

Once you click **Next**, Visual Studio will install the SQL Server Data Tools and once it is completed, you will get the following screen, which shows the setup completion status:

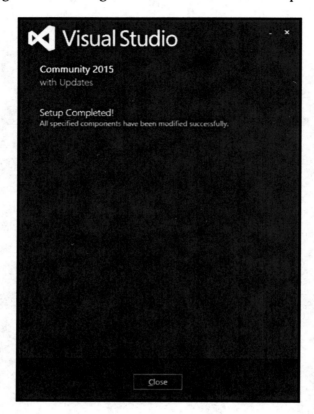

Deploying the ASP.NET Core application in Azure

Let's create an ASP.NET Core application that we can deploy in Microsoft Azure:

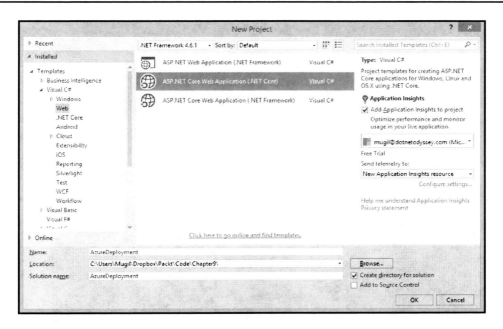

The ASP.NET Core application will be created once you click the **OK** button:

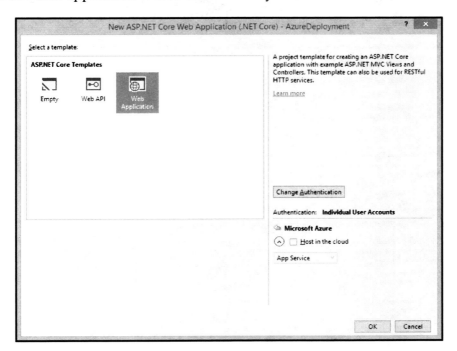

As the default ASP.NET Core Web Application template uses the Entity Framework, we need to execute the following command in order to create the database migration:

```
dotnet ef database update
```

Once you enter the command in **Command Prompt** (in the project's path), the migration file will be created. This migration file will contain all the changes to the database. This migration will be applied at the time of deployment at Azure so that Azure can create the necessary database scripts for Azure deployment:

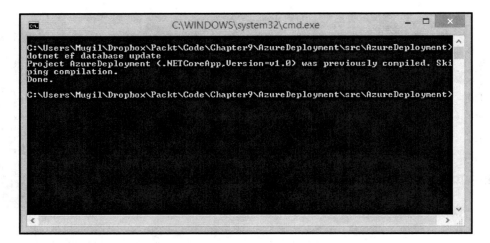

Once the database migration is completed, right-click on the created Core application and select the **Publish** option, as shown in the following screenshot:

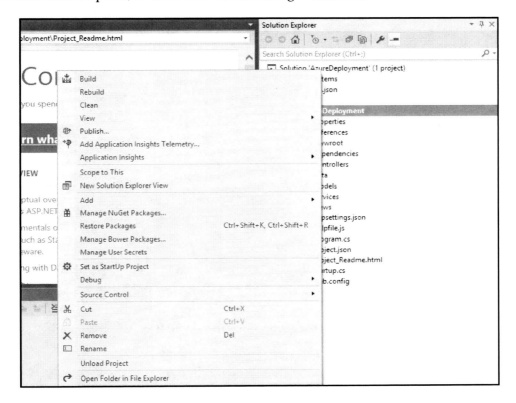

When you click the **Publish** option, you'll be shown the following screen, depicting various publishing options available for you:

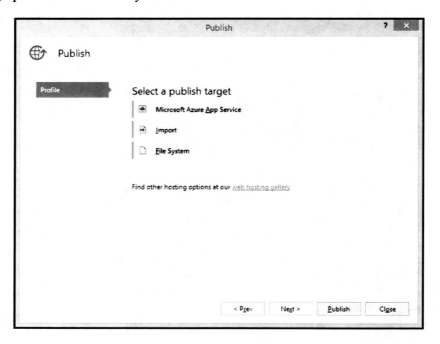

Please select the **Microsoft Azure App Service** option to publish the web application on the Microsoft Azure platform:

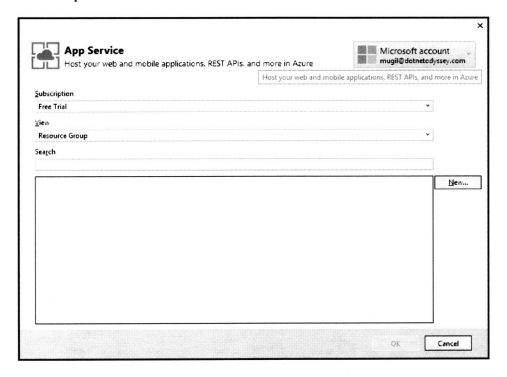

Click on the **New** button, and you will get the following screen:

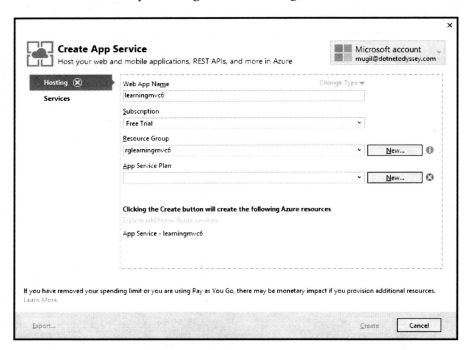

You can change the web app name to whatever name you would like to have. I have changed the web app name to **learningmvc6**.

Click on the **New** button beside the **Resource Group** and enter the name for the resource group. The resource group is just a tag where you can group all of your computing resources so that if you want to delete all the resources, you can just delete the resource group. For example, a resource group could comprise of a web server and a database server—you can think of it like a collection of resources.

Now, click on the **New** button beside the **App Service Plan**. You will get the following window where you can choose the location and size of your web application container. Your location could be anywhere from South Central US to Europe, from Japan to Canada. Your application container could be anything from free to a machine with 7 GB RAM. I have chosen the free option as our objective is to deploy the ASP.NET Core application in a cloud environment rather than to deploy an application which is to be accessed by millions of users. Of course, you can achieve the same with ASP.NET Core and Microsoft Azure:

Now, we can configure the SQL database which is available as an additional Azure service.

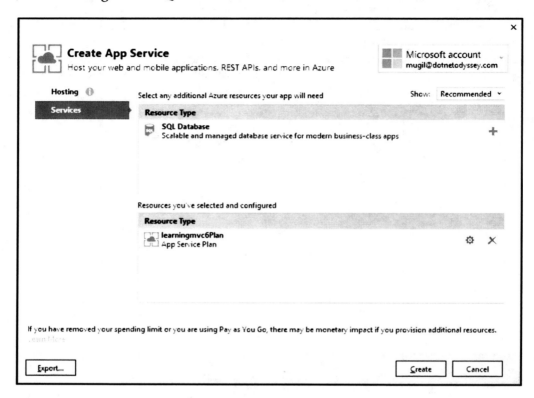

Click on the + button which is available at the top section which will lead us to the configuration of the SQL database.

If you have any existing SQL server in the Azure environment, you can use it. As I don't have any such server, I am going to create a SQL server by clicking the **New** button beside SQL Server:

Please enter the administrator user name and password for the SQL Server and click **OK**. You will see the following screen:

Once you click**OK**, you will get the following screen:

Click **OK** on the preceding screen and we will see the **Create App Service** screen:

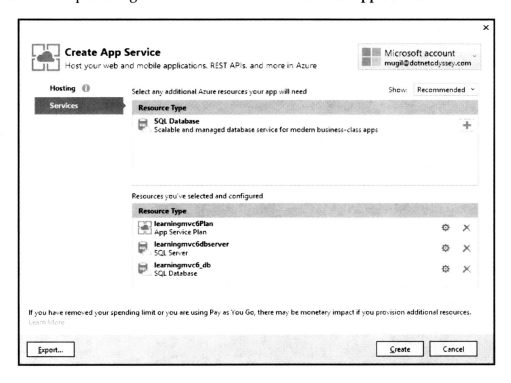

Click **Create** once we have configured all the required Azure services:

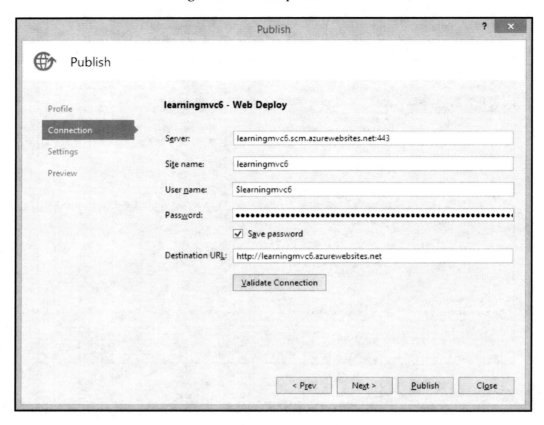

The preceding screen shows the deployment configuration options, such as the **Site name** and **Destination URL** for our application. Click **Next** on the preceding screen:

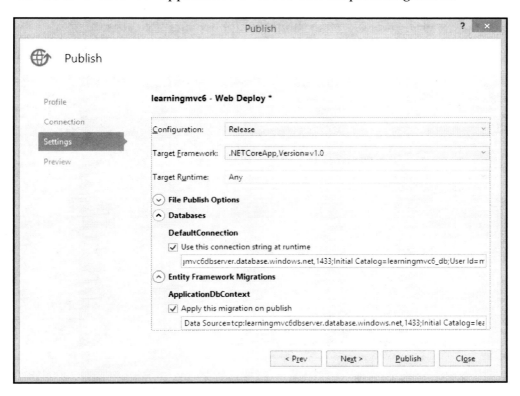

It is important to note that you need to expand the **Databases** option and **Entity Framework Migrations** options and select both the checkboxes. The first checkbox represents the connection string that should be used at runtime and the second checkbox represents the database migration that should be applied on publication.

The preceding screen is the preview screen where you can see the files that would be deployed when you publish. This is an optional step—if you want to see the files, you can click the **Start Preview** button. Or else, you can click the **Publish** button to publish the web application in the Azure platform.

Once you click the **Publish** button, our ASP.NET Core application will be deployed in Azure and your application URL will be opened on successful publication. You will get the following screen:

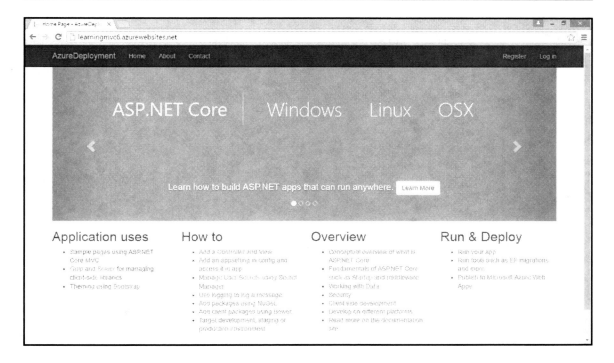

Deploying the ASP.NET Core web application in the Linux environment

In this section of the chapter, we are going to learn how to create and deploy the ASP.NET Core web application in the Linux platform. I am going to deploy the application in the cloud using **Amazon Web Services (AWS)**. Obviously, you don't need AWS to deploy the ASP.NET Core application on Linux. I am just using it so that I do not need to install Linux on my local machine. And another advantage of hosting with AWS (or any other public cloud service provider or any hosting provider) is that I can access the web application from anywhere as it will be publicly available.

We have the following prerequisites to create and deploy in the Linux environment:

- Linux machine
- Putty client (if you are using a remote Linux machine)

Creating a Linux machine

We are going to use AWS to create a Linux machine. The advantage of using AWS or any other cloud provider is that we can use their service only when we need it and we can wind down the machine when you are done with it. You only need to pay for the time when you are using it. For the first year, AWS has a free tier where you can host the machine (if it is eligible for the free tier) without having to pay anything. I have been using AWS for more than couple of years to try out many things in the cloud, hence I am not eligible for the free tier.

However, you can install Linux on your Windows PC by using any virtualization software. Ubuntu Linux has the option of booting up from the USB drive itself so that you don't need to disturb anything in your local PC.

Once you sign-up for an AWS account, you can go to the **EC2 dashboard**, where you can create **EC2 instances**:

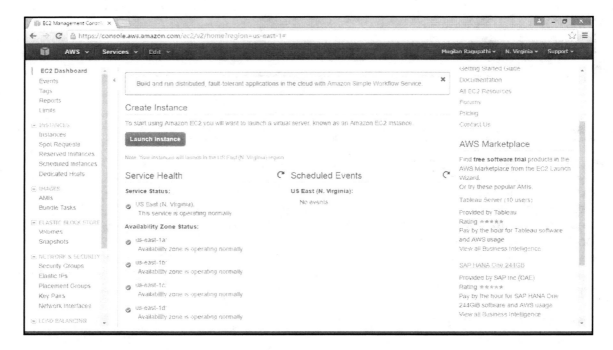

Click **Launch Instance** in the preceding screen. A wizard will be launched where it will help you in selecting and configuring the instances. In this step, we are selecting the Ubuntu Linux server because of its ease of use.

There are different kinds of instances available in AWS ranging from **nano** (with 0.5 GB RAM) to large machines (with 1952 GB RAM). We are going to choose **micro** instance as it is eligible for the free tier:

In previous step, we can configure the instances for the cloud. We can create an auto scale group where the AWS cloud will spin up the instances automatically when the load is high. As our objective is to create and deploy the ASP.NET Core web application, we are going to leave the default values as they are and click **Next: Add Storage** to move to the next screen:

The **micro** instances do not come with any external storage. Hence, we need to add the storage in order to use it. We have three options for storage to choose from: **General Purpose SSD, Provisioned SSD,** and **Magnetic SSD.** Out of the three, the **General Purpose SSD** is the storage that would be usually used.

When your application is making high input-output operations, the throughput may come down. But in the Provisioned SSD you can maintain the required throughput from the storage device. Magnetic storage is just an old type of storage. We are going to use the General Purpose 8 GB **Solid State Drive (SSD)** as it serves our purpose well.

If you are using multiple instances, you can tag them so that you can control the instances by using the tag name. As we are going to launch only one instance, I am just going to leave it blank and move on to the next step:

In this step, we can configure the security group for the instance—which ports should be opened for the incoming traffic. The general rule in any configuration is to only open up the ports what you need and nothing else. You also need to tell the IP (or its range) from where the machine could be accessed from. As it is a demo application, we are going to open ports 22, for **Secure Shell (SSH)**; for using PuTTY, and 80, for accessing the Core web application.

Once you have configured the Security Groups, click **Review and Launch**.

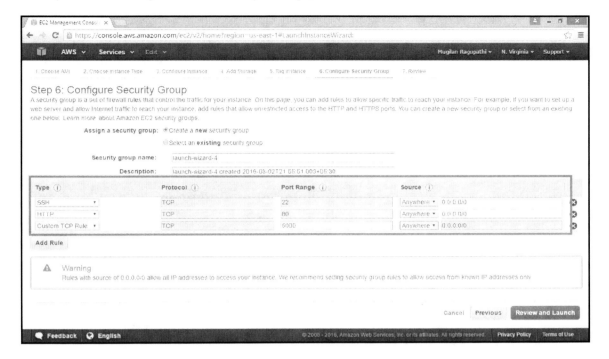

On the following screen, you can review the chosen options:

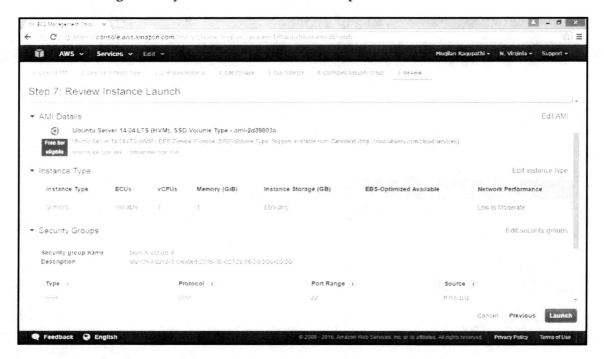

You can click **Launch** once you are fine with the selected options. Otherwise, you can go back to the previous step to reconfigure them with the correct values.

When you click **Launch**, it will ask you to choose a key pair which you will be using to log into any AWS server. If you do not have one, you can create one. As I have created one already, I am going to use the existing one, as shown in the following screenshot:

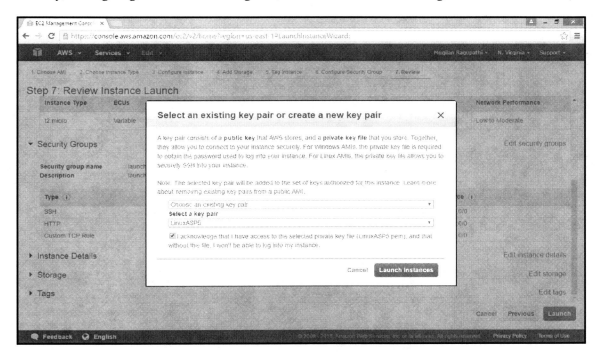

Select the key pair and click **Launch Instances**. AWS will spin up new instances for us and the status will be shown (as in the following screenshot). The instance ID will also be available (boxed in the screenshot):

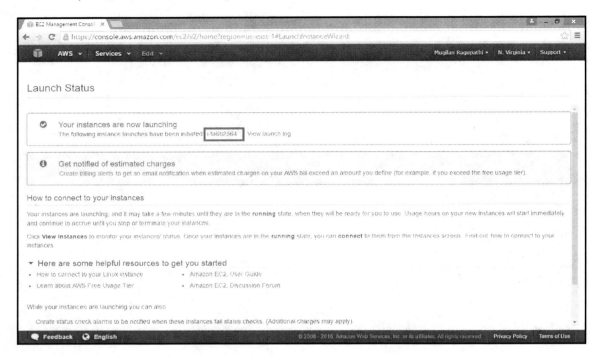

Clicking on the blue colored link will fetch you the status (as shown in the following screenshot). The **Public DNS** and **Public IP** are important values which you will be using to connect to that server. Hence, I've boxed them in the screenshot:

Installing the PuTTY client

Having created a new Linux server where we can create an ASP.NET 5 web application and host it, we need to install the PuTTY client, a small application that can send commands to the Linux server and receive the responses. As we are going to install the application in a Linux server, we need to have a way for connecting from your Windows PC to the Linux server. The PuTTY client application does exactly that.

You can download the PuTTY client by visiting `http://www.chiark.greenend.org.uk/~s gtatham/putty/`.

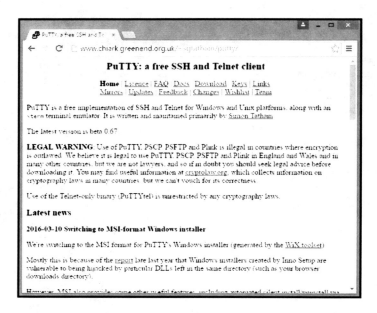

Click on the **Download** link and select the link (boxed in the screenshot) in the following screen:

It will download the MSI file. Once it's downloaded, launch the installer and you'll be shown the following welcome screen:

Click **Next** and you'll see following screen:

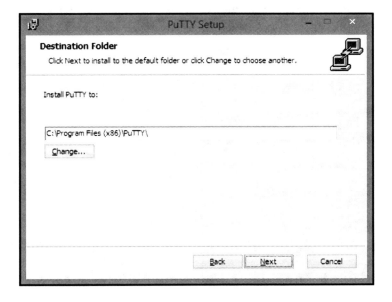

Choose the installation folder—you can leave it as it is and click **Next**:

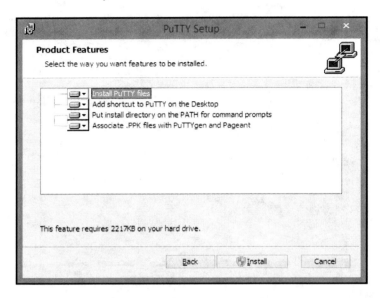

Select the product features which you want to install. You can leave the default selection and click **Install**. Once it is installed, you will be shown the following screen:

Click **Finish** and launch the PuTTY application. It will open the PuTTY configuration window, where we are going to enter the hostname and authentication details. The hostname is `<username>@<public DNS>`. In our case, it is **ubuntu@ec2-107-22-121-81.compute-1.amazonaws.com**. Ubuntu is the default user for the Ubuntu AMI that we have chosen. We can get the public DNS value in the status window as shown earlier:

For authentication, select **Connection | SSH | Auth** in the left-hand pane and select the PPK file (private key file) that we created earlier:

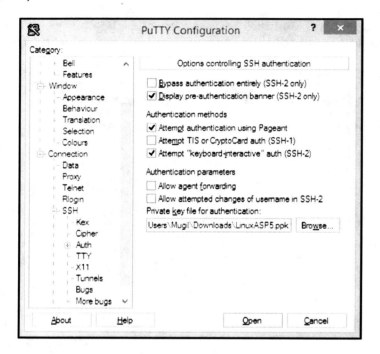

Click **Open**. You'll get a warning asking you whether you trust this host. Click **yes** and you'll be shown the Command Prompt of the Linux screen.

Next, we need to install .NET Core before creating the ASP.NET 5 application and eventually host them.

Installing of .NET Core in a Linux machine

In order to install .NET Core on Ubuntu, we need to first set up the apt and get feed that hosts the package that we need. Enter the following commands:

```
sudo sh -c 'echo "deb [arch=amd64]
https://apt-mo.trafficmanager.net/repos/dotnet-release/ trusty main" >
/etc/apt/sources.list.d/dotnetdev.list'

sudo apt-key adv --keyserver apt-mo.trafficmanager.net --recv-keys 417A0893
```

You will get the following screen:

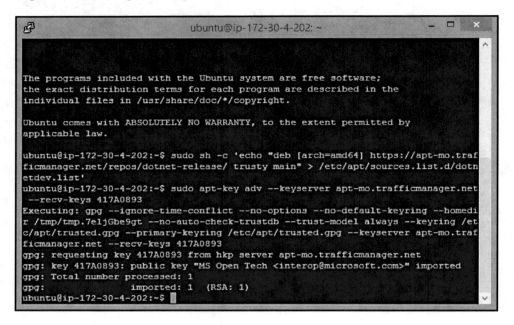

Then update it by issuing the following command, which will download the required packages and install them:

```
sudo apt-get update
```

You will see the following screen for this command:

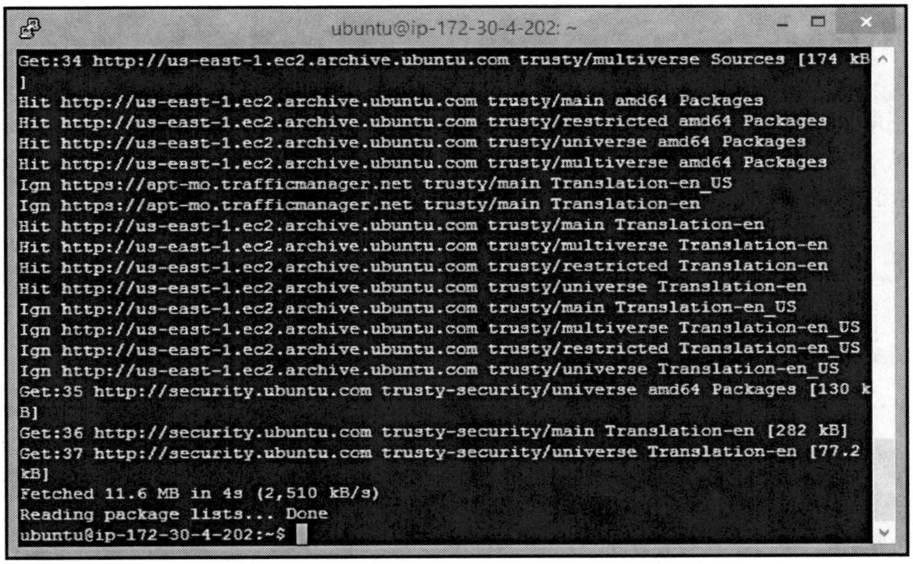

```
Get:34 http://us-east-1.ec2.archive.ubuntu.com trusty/multiverse Sources [174 kB
]
Hit http://us-east-1.ec2.archive.ubuntu.com trusty/main amd64 Packages
Hit http://us-east-1.ec2.archive.ubuntu.com trusty/restricted amd64 Packages
Hit http://us-east-1.ec2.archive.ubuntu.com trusty/universe amd64 Packages
Hit http://us-east-1.ec2.archive.ubuntu.com trusty/multiverse amd64 Packages
Ign https://apt-mo.trafficmanager.net trusty/main Translation-en_US
Ign https://apt-mo.trafficmanager.net trusty/main Translation-en
Hit http://us-east-1.ec2.archive.ubuntu.com trusty/main Translation-en
Hit http://us-east-1.ec2.archive.ubuntu.com trusty/multiverse Translation-en
Hit http://us-east-1.ec2.archive.ubuntu.com trusty/restricted Translation-en
Hit http://us-east-1.ec2.archive.ubuntu.com trusty/universe Translation-en
Ign http://us-east-1.ec2.archive.ubuntu.com trusty/main Translation-en_US
Ign http://us-east-1.ec2.archive.ubuntu.com trusty/multiverse Translation-en_US
Ign http://us-east-1.ec2.archive.ubuntu.com trusty/restricted Translation-en_US
Ign http://us-east-1.ec2.archive.ubuntu.com trusty/universe Translation-en_US
Get:35 http://security.ubuntu.com trusty-security/universe amd64 Packages [130 k
B]
Get:36 http://security.ubuntu.com trusty-security/main Translation-en [282 kB]
Get:37 http://security.ubuntu.com trusty-security/universe Translation-en [77.2
kB]
Fetched 11.6 MB in 4s (2,510 kB/s)
Reading package lists... Done
ubuntu@ip-172-30-4-202:~$
```

Install the .NET Core with the following command:

```
sudo apt-get install dotnet-dev-1.0.0-preview2-003121
```

The following screen will be displayed:

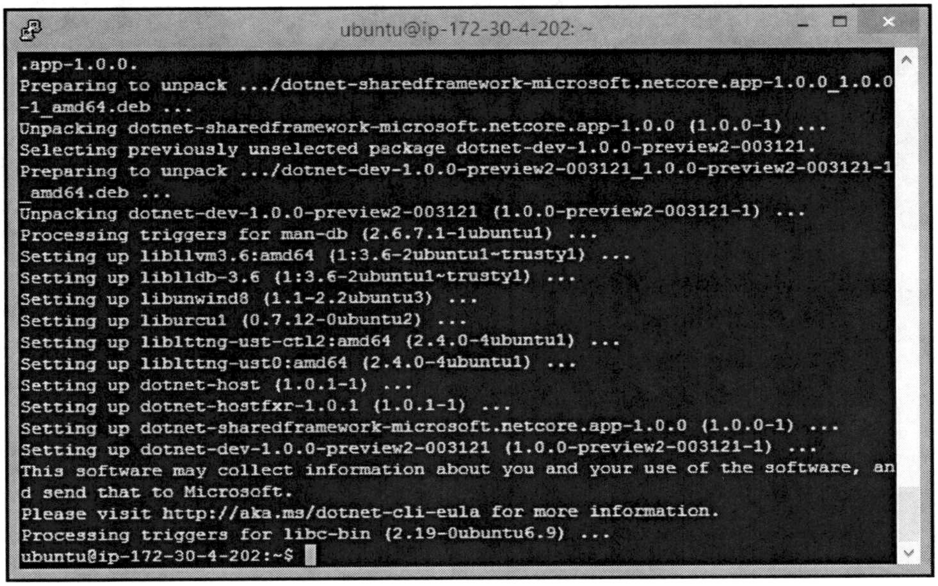

```
.app-1.0.0.
Preparing to unpack .../dotnet-sharedframework-microsoft.netcore.app-1.0.0_1.0.0
-1_amd64.deb ...
Unpacking dotnet-sharedframework-microsoft.netcore.app-1.0.0 (1.0.0-1) ...
Selecting previously unselected package dotnet-dev-1.0.0-preview2-003121.
Preparing to unpack .../dotnet-dev-1.0.0-preview2-003121_1.0.0-preview2-003121-1
_amd64.deb ...
Unpacking dotnet-dev-1.0.0-preview2-003121 (1.0.0-preview2-003121-1) ...
Processing triggers for man-db (2.6.7.1-1ubuntu1) ...
Setting up libllvm3.6:amd64 (1:3.6-2ubuntu1-trusty1) ...
Setting up liblldb-3.6 (1:3.6-2ubuntu1~trusty1) ...
Setting up libunwind8 (1.1-2.2ubuntu3) ...
Setting up liburcu1 (0.7.12-0ubuntu2) ...
Setting up liblttng-ust-ctl2:amd64 (2.4.0-4ubuntu1) ...
Setting up liblttng-ust0:amd64 (2.4.0-4ubuntu1) ...
Setting up dotnet-host (1.0.1-1) ...
Setting up dotnet-hostfxr-1.0.1 (1.0.1-1) ...
Setting up dotnet-sharedframework-microsoft.netcore.app-1.0.0 (1.0.0-1) ...
Setting up dotnet-dev-1.0.0-preview2-003121 (1.0.0-preview2-003121-1) ...
This software may collect information about you and your use of the software, an
d send that to Microsoft.
Please visit http://aka.ms/dotnet-cli-eula for more information.
Processing triggers for libc-bin (2.19-0ubuntu6.9) ...
ubuntu@ip-172-30-4-202:~$
```

Creating a new ASP.NET 5 project

Issue the following commands to create a new directory where we will create the ASP.NET 5 application. The first command (**mkdir** – make directory) is for creating a directory in Linux and the second command (**cd** – change directory) is for going inside the folder. And the last command is the command line to create a .NET Core application:

```
mkdir aspnetcoreapp
cd aspnetcoreapp
dotnet new
```

The following screen will be displayed:

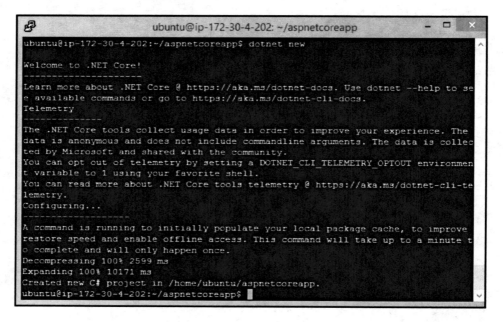

This will create the .NET Core application, which has a couple of files—Program.cs and project.json. It's a bare minimum application that does not have even Startup file.

We need to add the `Kestrel HTTP Server` package as a dependency in `project.json`. You can edit the file by issuing the command **vi project.json**. By default, the vi editor will open the file in read-only mode. You need to press *Esc + I* in order to make it to the edit mode. Add the line **"Microsoft.AspNetCore.Server.Kestrel": "1.0.0"** as shown in the following screenshot:

Press the Escape key and ":" and type `wq` to write into and quit the `vi` editor.

As we have added the dependency, we need to restore the packages by executing the following command:

```
dotnet restore
```

Once you enter this command, all the packages will be restored as shown in the following screenshot:

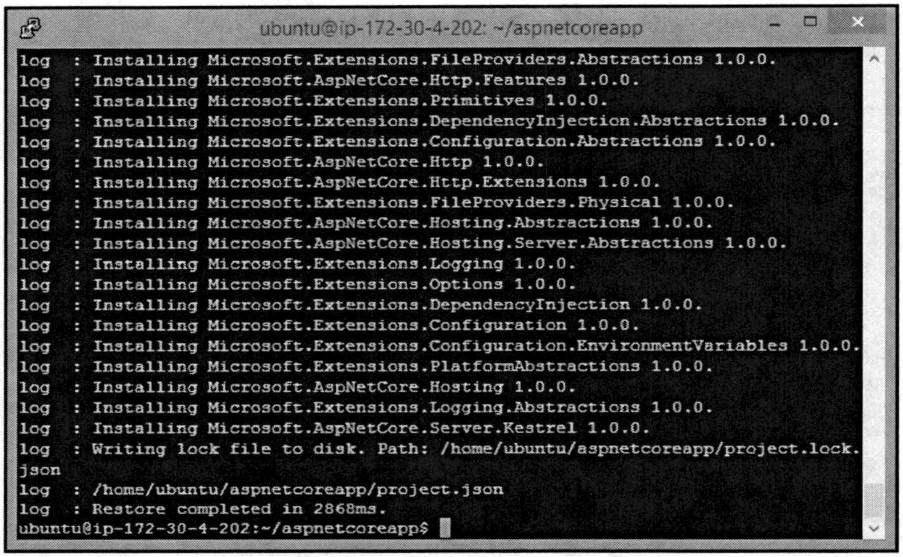

Create a new file, Startup.cs, with the following content. You can create a new file by issuing the command **vi Startup.cs**. As usual, we need to press *Esc + I* to make the file in write and read mode. Paste the following content (you can paste it by right-clicking on the mouse after copying it from here):

```
using System;
using Microsoft.AspNetCore.Builder;
using Microsoft.AspNetCore.Hosting;
using Microsoft.AspNetCore.Http;
namespace aspnetcoreapp
{
  public class Startup
  {
    public void Configure(IApplicationBuilder app)
    {
      app.Run(context =>
        {
            return context.Response.WriteAsync("This is ASP.NET Core
application running in Linux!");
        });
    }
  }
}
```

Press *Esc + :* and type `wq`, to save the file. Update the `Program.cs` file with the following content:

```
namespace aspnetcoreapp
{
  public class Program
  {
    public static void Main(string[] args)
    {
      var host = new WebHostBuilder()
      .UseKestrel()
      .UseStartup<Startup>()
      .Build();
        host.Run();
    }
  }
}
```

You'll see the following screen:

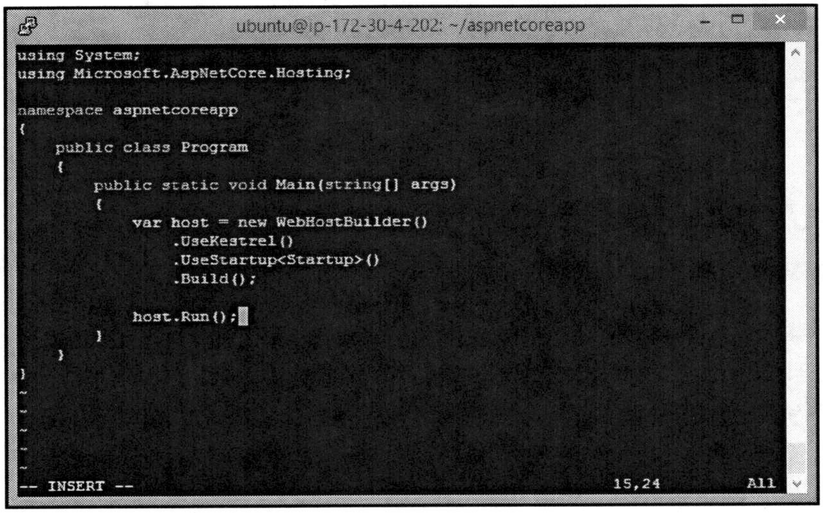

We have created the ASP.NET Core web application. Now we need to install **Nginx**, a reverse proxy server, which enables you to offload work such as serving static content, caching, and compressing requests. You can configure Nginx to listen on a particular port (we'll discuss the details later in this chapter). You can install Nginx by issuing the following command:

```
sudo apt-get install nginx
```

Once it is installed, you can issue the following command to start the service:

```
sudo service nginx start
```

When you'll run the command, you'll see the following screen:

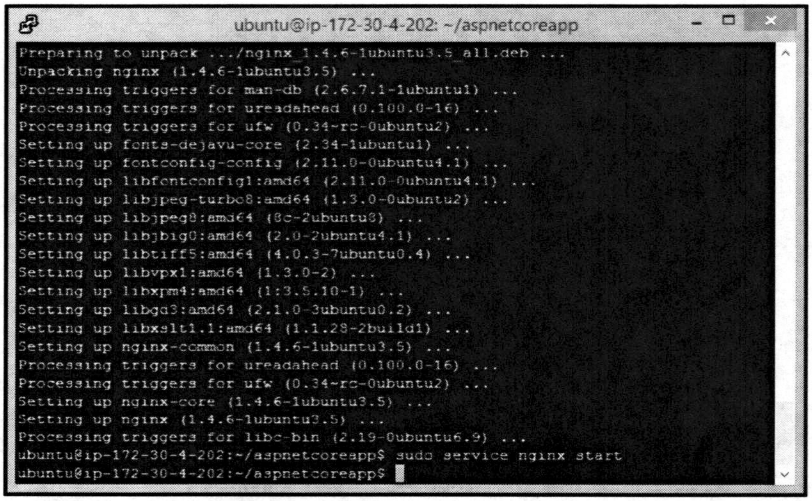

Configuring the Nginx server

Configure the Nginx server by modifying the file (/etc/nginx/sites-available/default) to have the following content—so that Nginx will forward the request to ASP.NET. In order to modify this file, you need to have sufficient rights—try switching to a super user. The Sudo su is the command for switching it to a super user. See the following code:

```
server {
  listen 80;
  location / {
    proxy_pass http://localhost:5000;
    proxy_http_version 1.1;
    proxy_set_header Upgrade $http_upgrade;
    proxy_set_header Connection keep-alive;
    proxy_set_header Host $host;
    proxy_cache_bypass $http_upgrade;
  }
}
```

The code looks like the following:

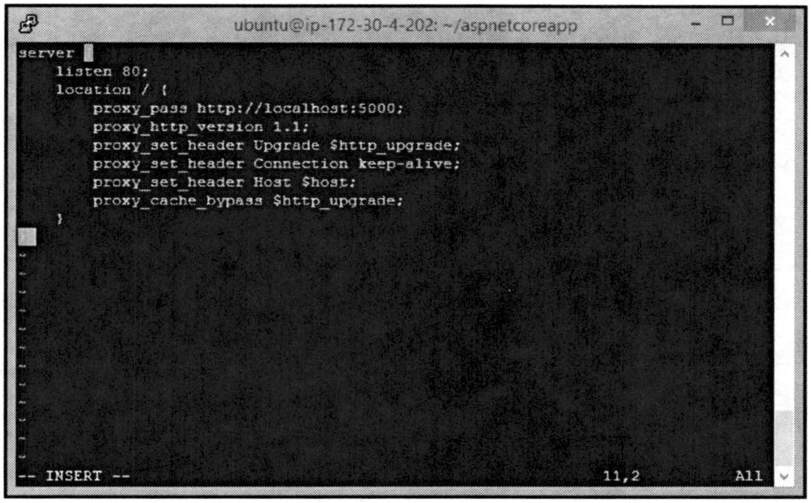

Run the application by executing the following command:

```
dotnet run
```

You will see the following screen:

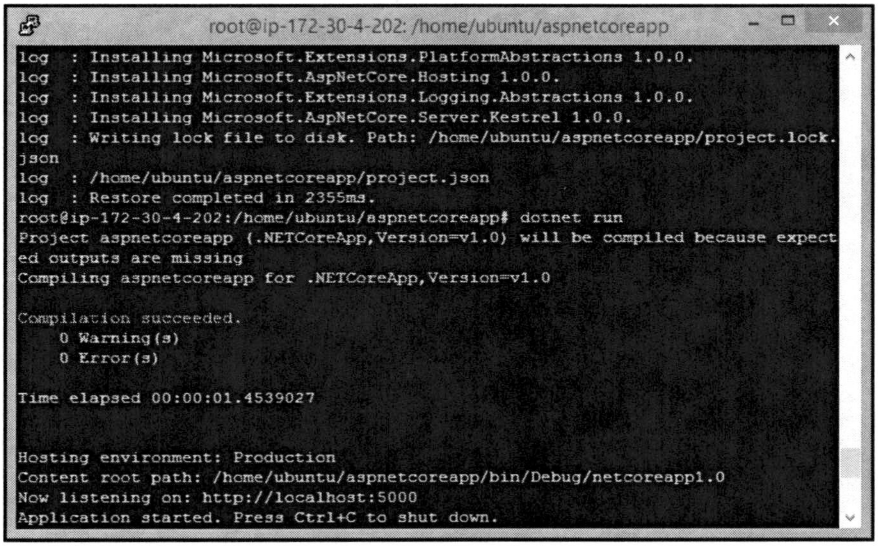

Now access the application from your browser using the public DNS (AWS created the public DNS when the instance was launched):

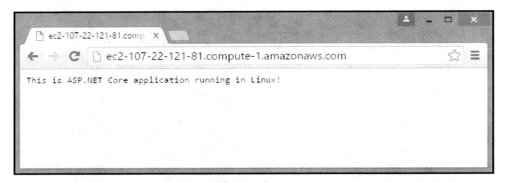

Voila! We have created the ASP.NET Core web application and launched it in the Linux box. We have even used the cloud through **Amazon Web Services** (**AWS**).

Summary

In this chapter, you have learned about the different components available in the `project.json` file, where all the configuration of your ASP.NET Core goes. We have discussed how to sign up to the Microsoft Azure cloud platform and deploy the ASP.NET Core application in the Azure platform. We have also learned how to create and deploy the ASP.NET Core web application in Linux using Amazon Web Services in the cloud.

10
Building HTTP-based Web Services Using ASP.NET Web API

So far, we have learned how to create web applications using ASP.NET Core. But there are times when simply creating a web application is not enough. Let's assume you are using ASP.NET Core to create a web application that provides weather information for all the cities across the world. People access your web application to find out weather information, and they are satisfied with the service. But this weather information may be needed by many other websites or web applications, such as tourism websites, news websites, and many other mobile applications.

Instead of writing the code all over again for their websites, you can create and publish the web services and the websites can consume the required web services whenever they need to.

In this chapter, you are going to learn about the following topics:

- What an HTTP-based service is and how it is useful
- What Fiddler is
- How to compose an HTTP request using Fiddler and fire the same in order to get an HTTP response
- How to design and implement the HTTP service using Web API

Microsoft provides ASP.NET Web API for programmers to build HTTP-based services. But HTTP is not just used to serve the webpages. You can use HTTP as a platform. This brings several advantages:

- As web services built using ASP.NET Web API use HTTP for communication, these web services can be consumed from all kinds of applications from console applications to web applications, and from WCF services to mobile applications
- Whenever there is any change in the logic/code of the web services, the clients (the websites that consume the services) do not need to change anything. They can consume the web services just as they were consuming them earlier

HTTP basics

HTTP is a powerful platform for building services. You can use the existing HTTP verbs to build services. For example, you can use the existing HTTP verb GET to get the list of products or POST to update information about the product. Let's take a quick look at how HTTP works with respect to building the services.

There is no difference in the underlying mechanism between serving the HTML pages in ASP.NET MVC and serving the data in the context of HTTP services. Both follow a request-response pattern and the same routing mechanism.

An HTTP request can be sent from any client (desktop, laptop, tablet, mobile, and so on) to the server and the server will respond back with an HTTP response. An HTTP response can be sent to the client in any format such as JSON or XML. This is shown in the following figure:

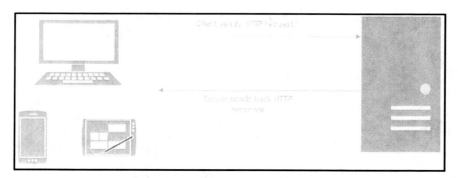

In the preceding diagram, a request is sent from the desktop computer (it could equally be sent from a mobile or tablet; it makes no difference) and the server sends back the HTTP response for the request. As HTTP is supported in most of the devices, it is ubiquitous.

HTTP verbs

HTTP verbs describe how the request has to be sent. These are the methods defined in HTTP that dictate how the HTTP requests are sent from the client to the server

GET method

When we use an HTTP GET request, the information is passed through the URL itself:

```
GET api/employees/{id}
```

This GET request gets the employee information based on the passed ID. The advantage of using the GET request is that it is lightweight, and all the required information will be passed in the URL or header itself, as shown in the following diagram:

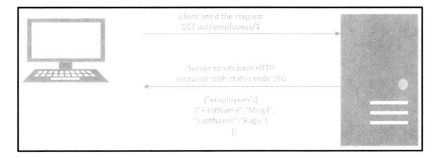

PUT method

The PUT method is used to create a resource or to update it. PUT is an idempotent operation, meaning that the expected behavior would not change even if it is executed multiple times:

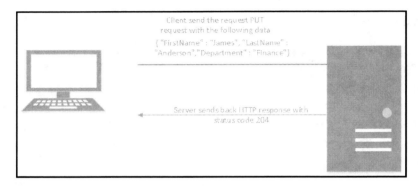

POST method

You can use POST to create or update the resource. Usually, POST is used to create the resource rather than update it. As per HTTP standards, whenever you create a new resource, you should return a **201 HTTP** status code:

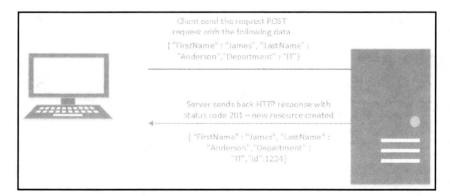

DELETE method

The DELETE method is used to delete the resource. Usually, when you delete a resource, you would be passing the ID as a parameter, and you would not be passing anything in the body of the request:

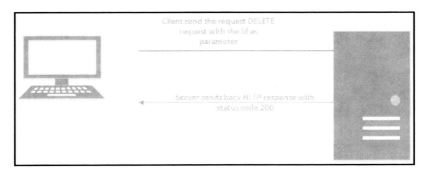

Usually, HTTP services would be consumed by other applications and services. Applications that consume services are referred to as clients. One of the options to test HTTP services is to build the clients. But this would be time-consuming, and we may throw away the client code once we test the HTTP services.

Another option, which is widely used, is to use applications that enable us to fire HTTP requests and monitor the responses. There are many applications available, Fiddler being one such widely used application.

Fiddler tool

Fiddler is the proxy server application used to monitor the HTTP and HTTPS traffic. You can monitor the requests that are being sent to the server from the client, the responses that are sent to the client, and the responses that are being received from the server. It is like seeing the traffic in the pipe between the server and the client. You can even compose a request, fire it, and analyze the response received without ever needing to write the client for the services.

You can download Fiddler at `http://www.telerik.com/fiddler`. You'll see the following window:

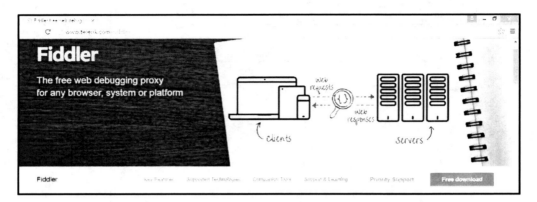

Enough theory. Let us create a simple web service using ASP.NET Web API.

Fire up Visual Studio 2015:

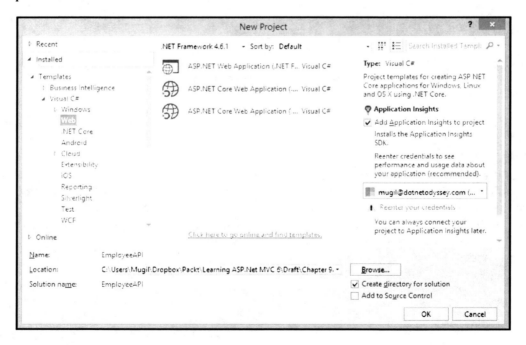

When you click **OK**, a Web API solution will be created. Just as the ASP.NET Core application controller inherits from the Controller class.

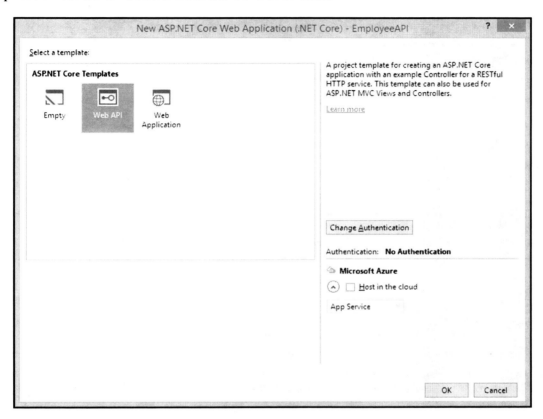

The Web API class will also inherit from the same Controller class. This is the difference between ASP.NET Core and earlier versions of ASP.NET MVC. In earlier versions, all Web API controller classes inherited from the `ApiController` class. In ASP.NET 5, it has been unified, and the same base Controller class is being used for both building web applications and services.

The following is the `ValuesController` class that will be created by default when you choose the **Web API** template option when creating the project:

Before we create our own custom Controller, let's analyze the default API Controller. In the `ValuesController` file, several API methods are already defined.

There are two overloaded `GET` methods—one with a parameter and another without a parameter. The `GET` method without a parameter returns all the resources of the type. In this case, we are returning just a couple of strings. In the real world, we would be returning the metadata of the resources. For example, if we fire the `GET` request on the movies API Controller, it would return information about all the movies. The `GET` method with an `id` parameter returns the resource whose ID matches with the passed ID. For example, if you pass a movie ID, it would return the information about that movie. The body of the other methods, such as `PUT`, `POST`, and `DELETE`, are empty in this Controller, and we will talk about these methods later.

When you run the application, you will get the following output:

By default, it fires a request to `api/values`, and the values are displayed in the browser.

Let's learn how to fire an HTTP request from the Fiddler application. Open the Fiddler application. In the bottom left-hand corner, select the **Web Browsers** option in the red box. Choosing this option will enable us to view the traffic coming from the **Web Browsers**:

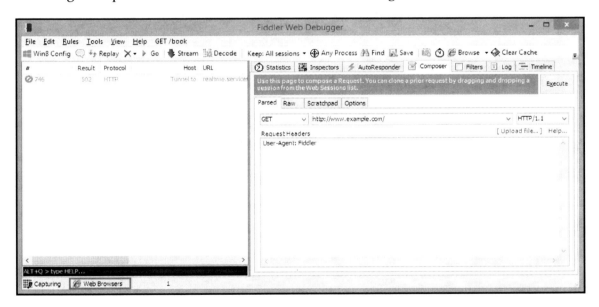

Select the **Composer** tab, enter the URL `http://localhost:49933/api/values`, as shown in the following screenshot, and click the **Execute** button in the top right-hand corner:

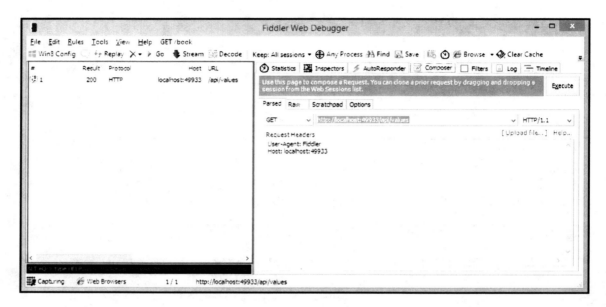

Once you click the **Execute** button, an HTTP session will be created, visible on the left-hand side pane (highlighted in the blue box). Click on the session and select the **Inspectors** tab on the top right-hand side pane. Select the JSON tab in the bottom right-hand side pane (highlighted by the purple-bordered box in the following screenshot).

You can see the JSON data returned from the HTTP request—**value1** and **value2** in the following screenshot:

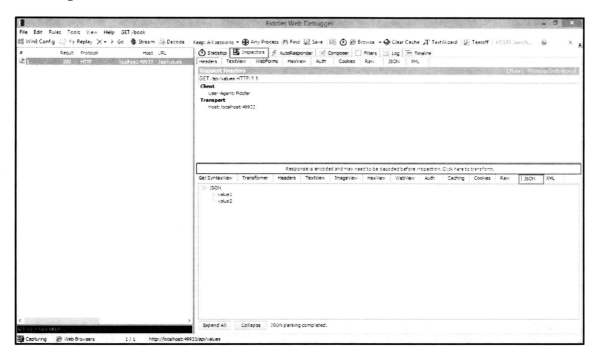

Now it's our turn to write a custom API.

In this custom API, we are going to provide API methods to create an employee object, list all the employee objects, and delete an employee object.

First, let us create a model for the employee. We need to create a folder to hold these models. Right-click on the project, select **Add** | **New folder**, and name the folder as `Models`:

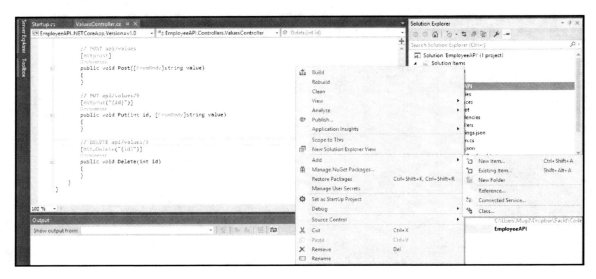

Right-click on the `Models` folder and select **Add** | **New Item...** to create an employee model class. This employee model class is just a POCO class. See the following code:

```
public class Employee
{
    public int Id {get; set;}
    public string FirstName {get; set;}
    public string LastName {get; set;}
    public string Department {get; set;}
}
```

Then, we define the repository interface to handle the model:

```
public interface IEmployeeRepository
{
    void AddEmployee(Employee e);
    IEnumerable<Employee> GetAllEmployees();
    Employee GetEmployee(int id);
    Employee RemoveEmployee(int id);
    void UpdateEmployee(Employee employee);
}
```

Then we implement the interface for this model:

```
public class EmployeeRepository : IEmployeeRepository
{
  private static List<Employee> employees = new List<Employee>();

  public EmployeeRepository()
  {

    Employee employee1 = new Employee
    {
      FirstName = "Mugil",
      LastName = "Ragu",
      Department = "Finance",
      Id = 1
    };

    Employee employee2 = new Employee
    {
      FirstName = "John",
      LastName = "Skeet",
      Department = "IT",
      Id = 2
    };

  employees.Add(employee1);
  employees.Add(employee2);
  }

  public IEnumerable<Employee> GetAllEmployees()
  {
    return employees;
  }

  public void AddEmployee(Employee e)
  {
    e.Id = GetNextRandomId();
    employees.Add(e);
  }

  public Employee GetEmployee(int id)
  {
    return employees.Where(emp => emp.Id == id).FirstOrDefault();
  }

  public Employee RemoveEmployee(int id)
  {
    Employee employee = employees.Where(emp => emp.Id ==
```

```
id).FirstOrDefault();
    if (employee !=null )
    {
      employees.Remove(employee);
    }
    return employee;
  }

  public void UpdateEmployee(Employee emp)
  {
    Employee employee = employees.Where(e => e.Id ==
emp.Id).FirstOrDefault();
    if(employee != null)
    {
    employee.Department = emp.Department;
    employee.FirstName = emp.FirstName;
    employee.LastName = emp.LastName;
    }
  }

  private int GetNextRandomId()
  {
    int id = -1;
    bool isIdExists;
    Random random = new Random();
    do
    {
      id = random.Next();
      isIdExists = employees.Any(emp => emp.Id == id);
    } while (isIdExists);
    return id;
  }
}
```

There are few things to be noted in the implementation class:

- We have decided not to use the database as our objective is to create an HTTP service using Web API, and not to write the data access code.
- We are using an in-memory list to hold the data. All the operations will be performed on this list. As a matter of fact, the data could be in any form, ranging from relational databases to a simple in-memory list.
- In the constructor method, we are adding an object to the list. This list will be acting as the database for our HTTP service.
- The `GetAllEmployees` API method will return all the employees as the `IEnumerable` interface.

- The `AddEmployee` method will add the employee (passed as a parameter) to the list.
- The `GetEmployee` method will return the employee whose ID matches that of the parameter.
- The `RemoveEmployee` method will remove the employee from the list.
- The `UpdateEmployee` method will update the employee information.
- The `GetNextRandomId` method will return the next available random integer. This integer value is being used to generate the employee ID.

Dependency Injection

In most real-world projects, we do not instantiate any objects using the `new` instance in any of the Controllers, the reason being that we don't want to have tight coupling between the dependent components (between the Controller and the repository). Instead, we pass an interface to the Controller, and the Dependency Injection container (such as **Unity**) will create an object for us when it is needed for the Controller. This design pattern is commonly referred to as **Inversion of Control**.

Let's say that a class by the name of *ClassA* uses another class, *ClassB*. In this case, it is enough for *ClassA* to know about the behavior, methods, and properties of *ClassB*, and it doesn't need the internal implementation details of *ClassB*. So, we can abstract *ClassB* and make an interface out of the class, and then have that interface as the parameter instead of the concrete class. The advantage of this approach is that we can pass any class at runtime as long as it implements a commonly agreed contract (interface).

In ASP.NET 5 (including ASP.NET Core and Web API), we have inbuilt support for Dependency Injection. In the `ConfigureServices` method, we have added the line (highlighted in bold) that performs the Dependency Injection. We instruct the inbuilt Dependency Injection container to create the `EmployeeRepository` class wherever we are referring to the `IEmployeeRepository` interface and we also instruct it to be a singleton; meaning that the same object (which is to be created by the Dependency Injection container) is to be shared for the entire lifecycle of the application:

```
public void ConfigureServices(IServiceCollection services)
{
  // Add framework services.
  services.AddApplicationInsightsTelemetry(Configuration);
  services.AddMvc();
  services.AddSingleton<IEmployeeRepository, EmployeeRepository>();
}
```

In the preceding code, we have used the Singleton pattern for the Dependency Injection, which creates services only the first time they are requested. There are other types of lifetime services such as **Transient** and **Scoped**. Transient lifetime services are created each time they are requested and Scoped lifetime services are created once per request. The following are code snippets created when you use such lifetimes:

```
services.AddTransient
  <IEmployeeRepository, EmployeeRepository>();

services.AddScoped
  <IEmployeeRepository, EmployeeRepository>();
```

Now it's time to get into the meat of the action creating the API controller. Right-click on the **Controllers** folder and select **Add | New Item**. Then select **Web API Controller Class** from the list, as shown in the following screenshot. Name your Controller, and click the **Add** button:

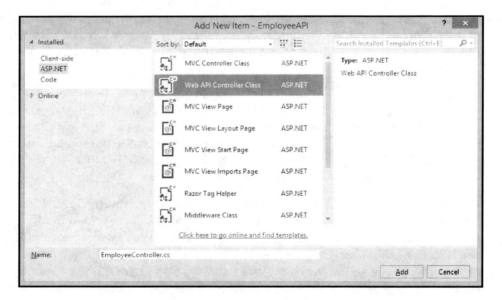

Remove the generated code in the Controller and add the following constructor:

```
public EmployeeController(IEmployeeRepository employeesRepo)
{
  employeeRepository = employeesRepo;
}
private IEmployeeRepository employeeRepository {get; set;}
```

In the preceding constructor, we are injecting the dependency. At the time of calling this constructor, the EmployeeRepository object will be created.

Let us implement a couple of GET methods—the first one will return all the employees' details and the second GET method will return the employee based on the passed employee ID:

```
public IEnumerable<Employee> GetAll()
{
   return employeeRepository.GetAllEmployees();
}

[HttpGet("{id}",Name ="GetEmployee")]
public IActionResult GetById(int id)
{
   var employee = employeeRepository.GetEmployee(id);
   if(employee == null)
   {
   return NotFound();
   }
   return new ObjectResult(employee);
}
```

Let us call these HTTP methods from Fiddler.

Run the solution, open the Fiddler application, and click on the **Composer** tab.

Select the HTTP method (we have chosen the GET method as we have a GET API method) and enter the URL http://localhost:49933/api/employee.

Please note that when I run my application, it runs on port 49933; the port number will be different in your case, so construct your URL accordingly.

Once you enter the URL and the method is selected, click the **Execute** button as shown in the following screenshot:

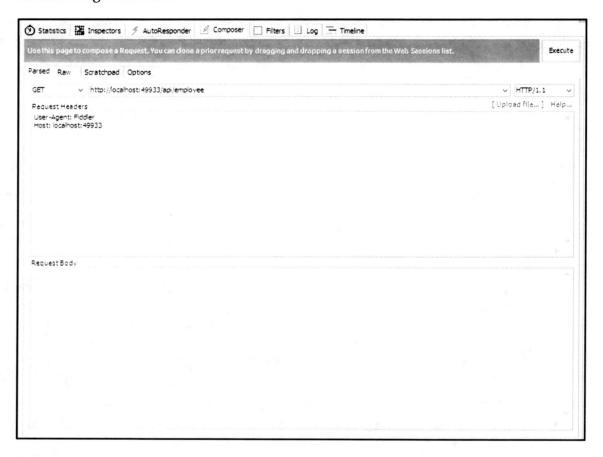

Once you click the **Execute** button, an HTTP session will be created, and the request will be fired.

Click on the session on the left-hand side pane (as shown in the following screenshot) and select the **Inspectors** tab in the right-hand side pane. You can view the result in the **JSON** tab in the bottom right-hand side pane:

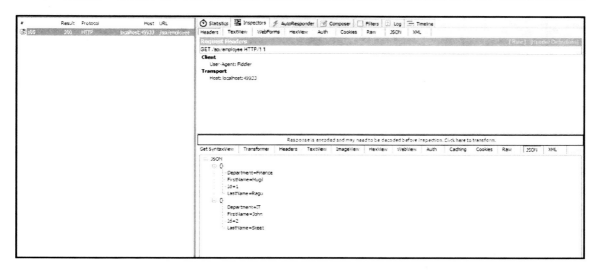

Let us fire another HTTP request to get a particular employee's information, say the employee whose ID is 2. We would construct the URL by appending the ID `http://localhost:49933/api/employee/2` as following:

Select the recently created HTTP session and click on it:

You can see the result in JSON format in the right-hand side pane.

Now, we are going to add `Create`, `Update`, and `Delete` operations to our service. To start with, we are going to provide the Create functionality to add employees' to our service:

```
[HttpPost]
public IActionResult Add([FromBody] Employee emp)
{
  if (emp == null)
  {
    return BadRequest();
  }
  employeeRepository.AddEmployee(emp);
  return CreatedAtRoute("GetEmployee", new { id = emp.Id }, emp);
}
```

The following points should be considered when following the preceding `Add` method:

1. We are passing the `Employee` object as a parameter. We are instructing the `Add` method to take that object from the body of the request by specifying a `[FromBody]` attribute:

    - If no employee object is passed, we would be returning the bad request to the calling client
    - If it is not null, we would be calling the repository method to add the employee to our list (in the real world, we would be adding it to the database)

2. Once we have added the employee, we are returning the *201 status code* (as per the HTTP standards) when a new resource is created.

Open the Fiddler application and follow these steps to add the employee:

1. Select the HTTP method as `POST` and enter the URL `http://localhost:54504/api/employee/`.
2. You need to specify the content type as `application/json` in the request header. Please see the following screenshot, where we have added `Content-Type: application/json` to the request header.

3. As mentioned in the code, we have to pass the employee object in the form of JSON in the body of the request. In the following request, we have formed a JSON that contains the properties of the `Employee` object with the values in the brackets { "FirstName" : "James", "LastName" : "Anderson","Department" : "IT"}:

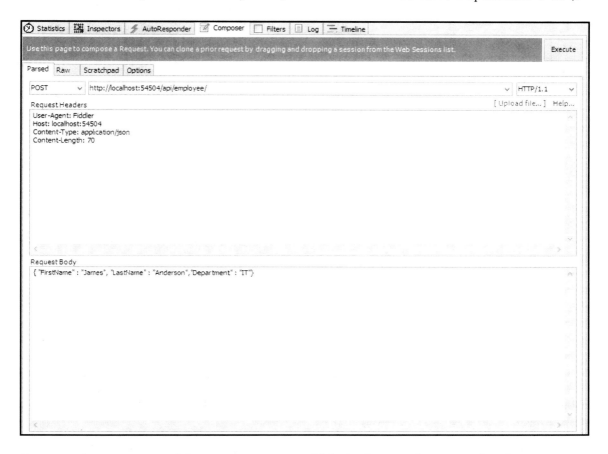

Once you have composed the request, you can click the **Execute** button to fire the request. This will return the *201 HTTP status code*, which is the standard HTTP response for creating a new resource:

As soon as we have created the resource in the server, we are redirecting the response to get the newly created resource. This occurs when we call the `CreatedAtRoute` method with the newly created employee ID passed as a parameter.

Click on the session on the left-hand side and select the **Inspector** tab in the right-hand side pane. Now you can see the response of the request. The response contains the `Employee` object which was newly created in the server. We have to note that the ID of the `Employee` object is generated at the server, and is available in the following response. In this case, the ID generated for the employee is `1771082655`:

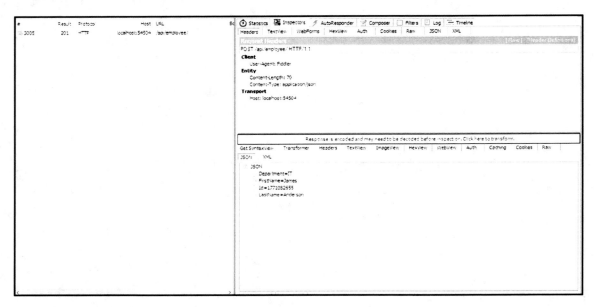

In the bottom right-hand side panel in the preceding Fiddler window, we can see the complete JSON response of the newly created resource.

Now we are going to add a Web API method to update the resource. The method for updating the resource is very similar to that used to create the resource, with only a few differences. When we created the resource, we used the HTTP POST method, whereas when we updated the resource, we used the HTTP PUT method.

If the passed employee ID could not be found in the repository, we return a *404 error response*, the HTTP standard error response for a resource that has not been found.

The following is the Web API controller method code for updating the resource:

```
[HttpPut]
public IActionResult Update([FromBody] Employee emp)
{
  if( emp == null)
  {
    return BadRequest();
  }
  Employee employee = employeeRepository.GetEmployee(emp.Id);
  if(employee == null)
  {
    return NotFound();
  }
  employeeRepository.UpdateEmployee(emp);
  return new NoContentResult();
}
```

The following is the repository layer code for updating the employee:

```
public void UpdateEmployee(Employee emp)
{
  Employee employee = employees.Where(e => e.Id ==
emp.Id).FirstOrDefault();
  if (employee != null)
  {
    employee.Department = emp.Department;
    employee.FirstName = emp.FirstName;
    employee.LastName = emp.LastName;
  }
}
```

Open the Fiddler application, and compose a request of HTTP PUT. As we are going to pass the Employee object in the body of the request, we need to mention the content type as application/json. In the body of the request, we need to supply the Employee object in JSON format, as shown in the following screenshot:

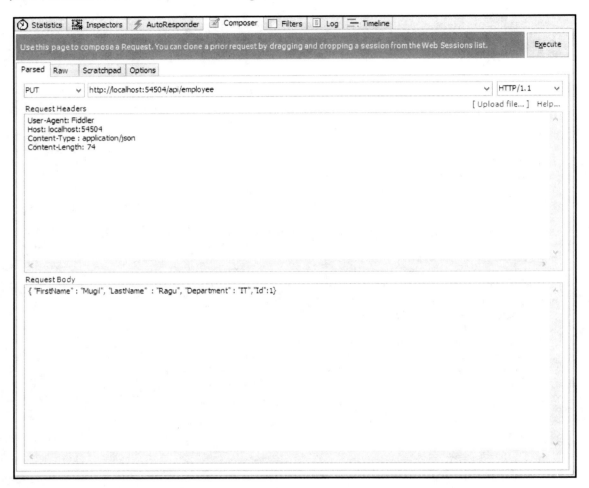

When you click the **Execute** button, the `HTTP PUT` request will be fired and our Web API method will get called. Once it succeeds, the *HTTP 204* response will be returned:

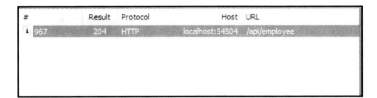

#		Result	Protocol		Host	URL
i	967	204	HTTP		localhost:54504	/api/employee

Delete method

The `HTTP DELETE` method should be used when deleting a resource. There is no need to pass anything in the body of the request.

The Web API method for deleting a resource

The `Delete` Web API method has a `void` return type, which will return an *HTTP 200* response:

```
[HttpDelete("{id}")]
public void Delete(int id)
{
   employeeRepository.RemoveEmployee(id);
}
```

Web Repository layer code for deleting the employee data

In the following repository layer method, we are removing the employee (whose ID matches with that of the parameter passed) from the internal list of employees. But in the real world, we would be interacting with the database to delete that particular employee. Consider the following code:

```
public Employee RemoveEmployee(int id)
{
   Employee employee = employees.Where(emp => emp.Id ==
id).FirstOrDefault();
   if(employee != null)
   {
     employees.Remove(employee);
```

```
    }
    return employee;
}
```

Open the Fiddler application, select the DELETE HTTP method, pass the URL with the parameter, and click on the **Execute** button. Please note that we are not passing the content type in the request header as we are not passing any employee object in the body of the request:

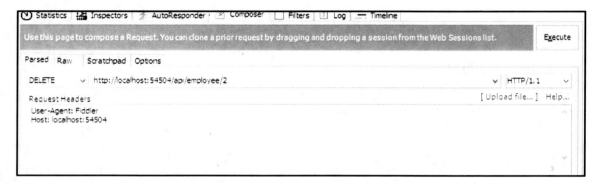

As we are returning void, the Web API DELETE method returns an *HTTP 200* status, as you can see in the left-hand side pane of the Fiddler application:

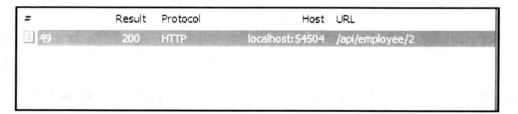

Summary

In this chapter, you learned about the HTTP service and its purpose. We discussed how to design and implement the HTTP service using Web API. We used the Fiddler tool to construct the HTTP request and get the response back. We also learned how to write the Web API method to perform CRUD operations end to end, from writing the Web API methods to firing the requests and getting the responses back.

11

Improving Performance of an ASP.NET Core Application

When you think about frequently accessed applications (the ones that we use daily), such as Google, YouTube, and Facebook, it is the performance of these applications that distinguishes them from similar applications. Think for a moment. If Google took more than 10 seconds to provide search results, most people would switch over to Bing or some other search engine. So, performance is one of the primary factors in an application's success.

In this chapter, we are going to learn about the following things:

- The approach to analyzing the performance issues of an application
- How to make use of browser developer tools to analyze the performance of an application
- Performance improvements in the UI layer
- Performance improvements in the web/application layer
- Performance improvements in the database layer

Normally, when people talk about the performance of an application, they think about the application's speed. Though speed contributes significantly to the performance of the application, we also need to consider maintainability, scalability, and reusability of the application.

A well-maintained code will be clear and have less technical debt, which in turn will increase the productivity of the developer. When we write code based on service-oriented architecture or micro services, our code will be more usable by others. This would also make our code scalable.

Normally, people think about the performance of the application when they have almost completed the development of the application and pilot users are complaining about the speed of the application. The right time to discuss performance is before the development of the application; we need to work with the product owners, business analysts, and actual users in order to arrive at a standard of an acceptable level of performance for the application. Then we design and code with this expected level of performance as our goal.

This also depends on the domain of the application. For example, a mission-critical healthcare application would demand great performance (they might expect responses in less than a second), whereas the performance of a back-office application may not demand so much. So, it is critical to understand the domain in which we are working.

If you have been asked to tune the performance of an existing application, it is also important to understand the existing architecture of the application. With ASP.NET Core, you can build a simple CRUD application to a mission-critical application serving millions of users across the world. A large application might have many other components, such as a load balancer, separate caching servers, **Content Delivery Networks (CDN)**, an array of slave DB servers, and so on. So, when you analyze the performance of the application, first you need to study architecture, analyze each of the individual components involved, measure the performance of each of the components, and try to optimize them when the application does not suit your acceptable performance. The main thing is not to jump into performance improvement techniques without studying and analyzing the architecture of the application. If you are creating a new application, you can think about performance right from the start of the application's creation.

We will examine a typical web application setup, shown in the following screenshot. We will then analyze it and consider how to improve it:

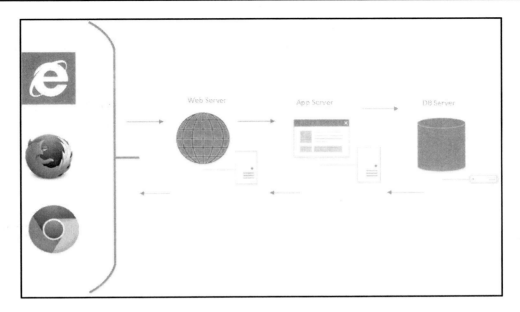

The following steps show the process of using a web application:

1. The user accesses an ASP.NET Core web application from a browser, such as Internet Explorer, Firefox, or Chrome. When the user types the URL into the browser and presses the *Enter* key, the browser creates a session and fires the HTTP request. This is not specific to an ASP.NET Core application. This behavior is the same for all web applications, irrespective of the technology on which they are built.

2. The request reaches the web server. If it is a simple request, the web server itself will serve that request. Serving a static HTML file is a typical example of this. If the request is a bit complex, for example, returning some data based on the business logic, the request will be forwarded to the application server.

3. The application server will query the database to get the data. Then it might do some business processing on the received data before returning the data to the web server. Sometimes, the web server might act as an application server for a smaller web application.

4. Then, the web server will return the response, typically in HTML, to the requesting client.

Thus, we can categorize these components into three layers—the UI layer, the web/application layer, and the DB layer. With respect to improving the overall performance of the ASP.NET Core application, we need to have a thorough look at how we can improve the performance of each of the layers.

Before implementing any performance improvement techniques, we need to first analyze the performance in each of the layers in the application. Only then can we suggest ways improve the overall performance of the application.

The UI layer

The UI layer represents all the events (and associated stuff) happening between the browser and the server. There are many events, including, but not limited to, the following:

- Firing the HTTP request
- Getting the response
- Downloading the resources
- Rendering them in the browser
- Any JavaScript code execution

Reducing the number of HTTP requests

A typical web page might not have only HTML content. It may have references to CSS files, JS files, and images, or other sources. So, when you try to access a web page, the client will fire HTTP requests for each of these references and download those references from the server to the client.

Browser developer tools come in handy when you want to analyze the HTTP requests being fired from the client. Most of the browsers have developer tools that you can make use of.

When you press *F12* in Internet Explorer, the **Developer Tools** window will open at the bottom of the Internet Explorer window, as shown in the following screenshot:

Click on the **Network** tab. Before entering the URL in the browser, click the *Start* button (the green play button), or click the green play button and refresh the page:

Once you press the **Network** tab's start button, Internet Explorer's **Network** tab will listen to each of the requests that are fired from the current tab. Each request will contain information, such as the URL, protocol, method, result (the HTTP status code), and other information.

I ran the application again with (**Tracking Network Requests** option ON) and I could see the requests being tracked, as shown in the following screenshot:

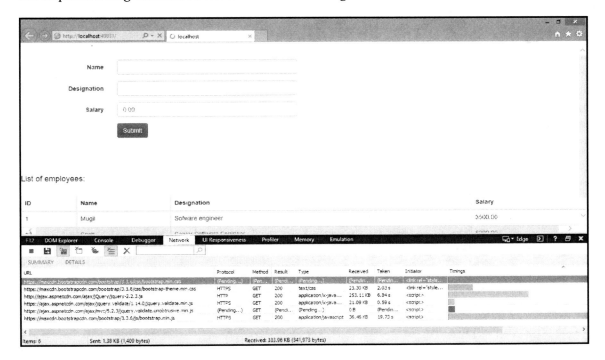

There are many useful pieces of data available in the Network tab. To begin with, the URL column shows the resource that is being accessed. The Protocol column, as the name implies, shows the protocol being used for accessing the resource.

To begin with, the URL column shows the resource that is being accessed. The Protocol column, as the name implies, shows the protocol being used for accessing the resource. The Method column shows the type of request, and in the Result column, we can see the HTTP status code of the request (HTTP 200 response means a successful GET request).

The Type column shows the type of resource that is being accessed, and the Taken column shows how much time it has taken to receive the file from the server. The Received column shows the size of the file that was downloaded as part of the request.

Using GZip compression

When you are serving the content, you can compress the content using GZip so that a smaller amount of data will be sent across the wire. You need to add the appropriate HTTP headers so that the browser can understand the mode of content being delivered. In IIS, this option is enabled for static resources by default. You can verify this by accessing the `applicationHost.config` file at the path `C:\Windows\System32\inetsrv\config`:

```
<httpCompression directory="%SystemDrive%\inetpub\temp\IIS Temporary
Compressed Files">
  <scheme name="gzip" dll="%Windir%\system32\inetsrv\gzip.dll" />
  <staticTypes>
    <add mimeType="text/*" enabled="true" />
    <add mimeType="message/*" enabled="true" />
    <add mimeType="application/x-javascript" enabled="true" />
    <add mimeType="application/atom+xml" enabled="true" />
    <add mimeType="application/xaml+xml" enabled="true" />
    <add mimeType="*/*" enabled="false" />
  </staticTypes>
</httpCompression>
```

If it is not available in your `applicationHost.config` file, you have to make the necessary changes.

Using the Content Delivery Network (CDN)

A Content Delivery Network is a system of distributed servers situated across the globe to serve the content based on the geographical location from where the content is accessed. Amazon's **CloudFront** is one example of a CDN. Amazon has edge locations (locations where servers are located) all over the world so that content can be served to users from the nearest location.

In the following line, we are accessing the jQuery from the CDN provided by the official jQuery website:

```
<script src="https://code.jquery.com/jquery-3.1.1.min.js" ></script>
```

Using JavaScript wherever possible

If you can use JavaScript to achieve a functionality, then do it. For example, before validating the data of the form on the server, always try to do client-side validation first. This approach has a couple of advantages—the site will be very fast, as everything is done at the client-side itself, and the server would handle a larger number of requests, as some of the requests are handled on the client-side.

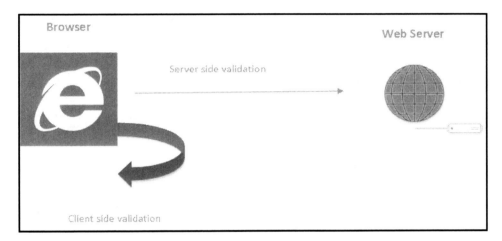

Using CSS stylesheets

As the browser renders the web page progressively (the browser will display whatever content it has, as soon as it receives it), it is better to place the stylesheets at the top rather than at the end of the web page. If we place the stylesheets at the bottom, it prohibits the progressive rendering as the browser has to redraw the content with the styles.

Most of the browsers will block parallel downloads when it comes to downloading the JavaScript files, so it is better to place the script at the bottom. This means that your content is shown to the user while the browser downloads the scripts. The following is the sample layout file created in an ASP.NET Core application where CSS files are referenced at the top and JavaScript files are referenced at the bottom:

```
<!DOCTYPE html>
<html lang="en">
  <head>
    <meta name="viewport" content="width=device-width" />
    <title>@ViewBag.Title</title>
    <!-- Latest compiled and minified CSS -->
```

```
    <link rel="stylesheet"
href="https://maxcdn.bootstrapcdn.com/bootstrap/3.3.6/css/bootstrap.min.css
"
integrity="sha384-1q8mTJOASx8j1Au+a5WDVnPi2lkFfwwEAa8hDDdjZlpLegxhjVME1fgjW
PGmkzs7" crossorigin="anonymous">

    <!-- Optional theme -->

    <link rel="stylesheet"
href="https://maxcdn.bootstrapcdn.com/bootstrap/3.3.6/css/bootstrap-theme.m
in.css" integrity="sha384-
fLW2N01lMqjakBkx3l/M9EahuwpSfeNvV63J5ezn3uZzapT0u7EYsXMjQV+0En5r"
crossorigin="anonymous">

  </head>
  <body>
    <div>
      @RenderBody()
    </div>
    <script
src="http://ajax.aspnetcdn.com/ajax/jQuery/jquery-2.2.3.js"></script>

    <script
src="https://ajax.aspnetcdn.com/ajax/jquery.validate/1.14.0/jquery.validate
.min.js"></script>

    <script
src="https://ajax.aspnetcdn.com/ajax/mvc/5.2.3/jquery.validate.unobtrusive.
min.js"></script>

    <!-- Latest compiled and minified JavaScript -->
    <script
src="https://maxcdn.bootstrapcdn.com/bootstrap/3.3.6/js/bootstrap.min.js"
integrity="sha384-0mSbJDEHialfmuBBQP6A4Qrprq5OVfW37PRR3j5ELqxss1yVqOtnepnHV
P9aJ7xS" crossorigin="anonymous"></script>

  </body>
</html>
```

Minification of JavaScript and CSS files and their combination

The time taken to download the related resources of a web page is directly proportional to the size of the files that are downloaded. If we reduce the size of the file without changing the actual content, it will greatly increase the performance. Minification is the process of changing the content of the file in order to reduce the size of the file. Removing the extraneous white spaces and changing the variable names to shorter names are both common techniques used in the minification process.

Popular JavaScript libraries such as jQuery and frontend frameworks provide minified files by default. You can use them as they are. In the following screenshot, I have downloaded the compressed version of jQuery. You can minify the custom JavaScript and CSS files that you have written for your application:

Bundling is the process where you can combine two or more files into one. Bundling and minification, when used together, will reduce the size of the payload, thereby increasing the performance of the application.

You can install the **Bundler & Minifier** Visual Studio extension from the following URL:

```
https://visualstudiogallery.msdn.microsoft.com/9ec27da7-e24b-4d56-8064-fd7e8
8ac1c40
```

Once you have installed this Visual Studio extension, you can select the files that you want to bundle and minify by selecting the files and selecting the **Bundler & Minifier** option from the **Context** menu, brought up by right-clicking. It is shown in the following screenshot:

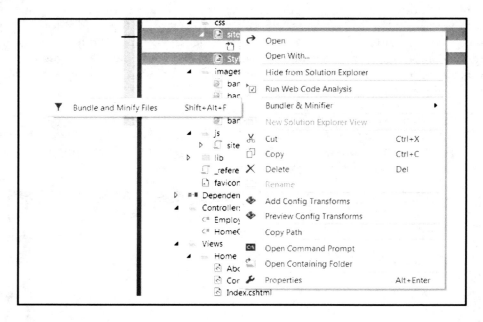

Once you select the **Bundle and Minify Files** option, it will ask you to save the bundled file as shown in the following screenshot:

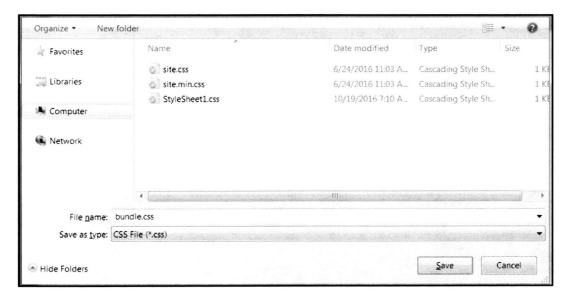

You can name the file of your wish and save the file. Once you save the file, another file would have been created in your solution—in our case, it is the `bundleconfig.json` file:

This file will have the information on the input files and the bundled output file. The following is one such example:

```
[
  {
    "outputFileName": "wwwroot/css/site.min.css",
    "inputFiles": [
    "wwwroot/css/site.css"
    ]
  },
```

```
{
  "outputFileName": "wwwroot/js/site.min.js",
  "inputFiles": [
  "wwwroot/js/site.js"
  ],
  "minify": {
  "enabled": true,
  "renameLocals": true
  }
},

{
  "outputFileName": "wwwroot/css/bundle.css",
  "inputFiles": [
  "wwwroot/css/site.css",
  "wwwroot/css/StyleSheet1.css"
    ]
  }
]
```

You can use this bundled file in your application, resulting in increased performance.

The caching process

Caching is the process of copying the data and having it in memory instead of getting the data again through an external resource, such as a network, file, or database. The data used in caching is ephemeral and can be removed at any time. As we are directly accessing the data, caching can greatly improve the performance of the application.

Caching can be done in any of the layers—client-side at the browser, at the proxy server (or at some middleware), or at the web/application server. For database layer caching, we might not need to do any custom coding. Based on the type of database server being used, you might need to make some configuration changes. However, most of the databases these days are powerful enough to cache the data as and when it is needed.

Client-side caching

We can cache at the client-side if we add the appropriate HTTP response headers. For example, if we want to cache all the static assets, such as CSS, images, and JavaScript files, we can add the **max-age** response header in the **Cache-Control** header:

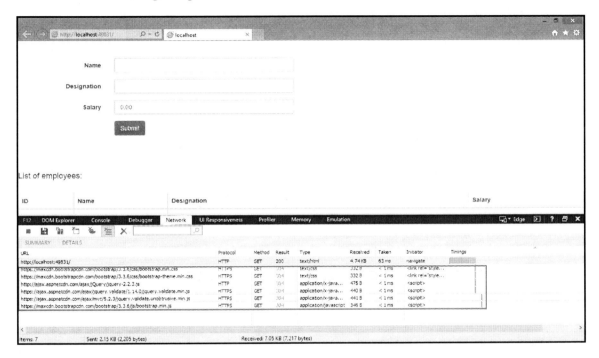

In the preceding screenshot of the **Developer Tool** window's **Network** tab, when the requests are fired again, we get *HTTP 304 response* (Not modified) as the response. This means the same files are not transferred back twice across the wire, as they are available in the browser itself.

Implementing browser caching for static files is pretty easy, and it involves just a couple of steps—adding dependencies and configuring the application.

Add the following NuGet package to the list of dependencies in the project.json file:

```
"Microsoft.AspNet.StaticFiles": "1.0.0-rc1-final"
```

Add the following namespaces to the `Startup.cs` file and configure the application to use those static files:

```
using Microsoft.AspNet.StaticFiles;
using Microsoft.Net.Http.Headers;

public void Configure(IApplicationBuilder app)
{
  app.UseIISPlatformHandler();
  app.UseMvc();
  app.UseMvc(routes =>
  {
    routes.MapRoute(name:"default",
template:"{controller=Employee}/{action=Index}/{id?}");});

    app.UseStaticFiles(new StaticFileOptions()
    {
      OnPrepareResponse = (context) =>
    {
      var headers = context.Context.Response.GetTypedHeaders();
      headers.CacheControl = new CacheControlHeaderValue()
      {
        MaxAge = TimeSpan.FromSeconds(60),
      };
      }
  });
}
```

Response caching

In response caching, cache-related HTTP headers are added to HTTP responses when MVC actions are returned. The Cache-Control header is the primary HTTP header that gets added to the response.

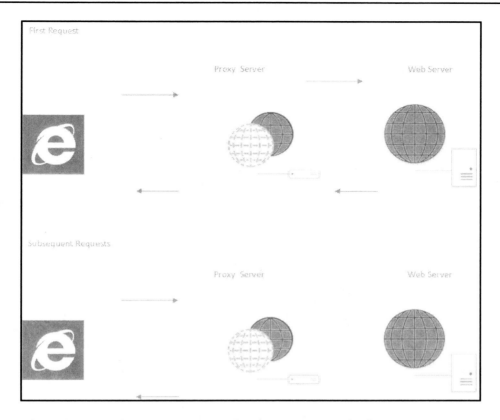

The preceding diagram shows response caching in action. In the first request, we are calling a Controller's action method; the request comes from the client and passes through the proxy server, actually hitting the web server. As we have added a response cache, any subsequent requests will not be forwarded to the web server, and the responses will be returned from the proxy server itself. This will reduce the number of requests to the web server, which in turn will reduce the load on the web server.

Caching the response of the Controller's action method is pretty easy. Just add the `ResponseCache` attribute with a duration parameter. In the following action method, we have added the response cache with a duration of 60 seconds, so that, for the next 60 seconds, if any requests come again, the responses will be returned from the proxy server itself instead of going to the web server:

```
[ResponseCache(Duration = 60)]
public IActionResult Index()
{
    EmployeeAddViewModel employeeAddViewModel = new    EmployeeAddViewModel();
    using (var db = new EmployeeDbContext())
```

```
  {
     employeeAddViewModel.EmployeesList = db.Employees.ToList();
  }
  return View(employeeAddViewModel);
}
```

The web/application layer

The web/application layer is composed of whatever happens between receiving the request from the client and sending back the response (or querying the DB layer to get the required data). Most of the web/application layer will be in a server-side language, such as C#, so when you try to optimize the web/application layer, you need to incorporate the best practices of ASP.NET MVC and C#.

No business logic in Views

A View is what is rendered to the browser, and it can contain presentation logic. Presentation logic represents where and how the data is to be displayed. ViewModels (actually, models specific to the View) are models that hold the data for a particular view.

Neither Views nor ViewModels should contain any business logic as this violates the separation of concerns principle.

Look at the following Razor View code. We are just looping through the list in the model and presenting the data in tabular format—nothing else:

```html
<h4> List of employees:</h4> <br />
  <table class="table table-bordered">
  <tr>
    <th> ID </th>
    <th> Name </th>
    <th> Designation </th>
    <th> Salary </th>
  </tr>
  @foreach (var employee in Model.EmployeesList)
  {
  <tr>
    <td>@employee.EmployeeId</td>
    <td>@employee.Name</td>
    <td>@employee.Designation</td>
    <td>@employee.Salary</td>
  </tr>
  }
```

```
            </table>
```

In some code, there might be a repository layer in ViewModel, which should never be the case. Please be extra cautious about what is there in the View/ViewModel code.

Using asynchronous logging

Try to use asynchronous logging, wherever possible, to improve the performance. Most logging frameworks, such as **Log4Net**, provide an option for logging asynchronously. With respect to the ASP.NET Core, you can implement the logging through a Dependency Injection.

The following is a typical example of the implementation of a logging framework in an MVC Controller:

```
public class EmployeeController : Controller
{
  private readonly IEmployeeRepository _employeeRepo;
  private readonly ILogger<EmployeeController> _logger;
  public EmployeeController(IEmployeeRepository employeeRepository,
  ILogger<EmployeeController> logger)
  {
    _employeeRepo = employeeRepository;
    _logger = logger;
  }
  [HttpGet]
  public IEnumerable<Employee> GetAll()
  {
    _logger.LogInformation(LoggingEvents.LIST_ITEMS, "Listing all
employees");
    return _employeeRepo.GetAll();
  }
}
```

The DB layer

Though the DB layer is not directly related to ASP.NET Core applications, it is the developer's responsibility to take complete ownership of the application's performance, and that includes taking care of the database's performance as well. We will now look at a few of the areas in the DB layer that we need to consider when improving the performance of an ASP.NET Core application.

Understanding the queries generated by the ORM

In most applications these days, we use **Object-Relational Mapping (ORM)**, such as Entity Framework or **NHibernate**. As you might know, the primary objective of the ORM is to enable you to write the data access layer using domain-based classes and objects instead of writing queries directly. However, it does not mean that you never need to understand the basics of the SQL queries generated, or the optimization of these queries. Sometimes, the generated query from Entity Framework may not be optimized, so a better practice would be to run the profiler, analyze the generated queries, and tune them as per your needs. You can use the interceptors in Entity Framework to log the SQL queries.

Using classic ADO.NET if you really want to

ASP.NET Core is just a web development framework, and it is not tied to any data access framework or technology. If the ORM that you use in your application does not support the performance that you expect it to, you can use the classic ADO.NET and manually write the queries/stored procedures.

Return only the required data

Always return only the data that you need nothing more, nothing less. This approach reduces the data that we send across the wire (from the database server to the web/application server).

For example, we would not use the following:

```
Select * from employees
```

Instead, we would use this:

```
Select FirstName,LastName from employees
```

The latter query would get only the required fields from the table, and, thus, only the required data is passed across to the calling client.

Fine tuning the indices

Beginners tend to add indices whenever they face a problem with the database. Adding an index to every column in the table is bad practice, and will reduce performance. The right approach is to take the list of queries that are most frequently executed. Once you have this list, try to fine tune them—remove unnecessary joins, avoid correlated subqueries, and so on. Only when you have tried and exhausted all query tuning options at your end should you start adding the indices. The important thing to note here is that you should add indices only on the required number of columns.

Using the correct column type and size for your database columns

When you want to use int as a datatype for a column, use an integer. Don't use double. This will save a lot of space if you have lots of rows in your table.

Avoiding correlated subqueries

Correlated subqueries use values from their parent query, which in turn makes it run row by row. This would significantly affect the query performance.

The following is one such example of a correlated subquery:

```
SELECT e.Name,
e.City,
(SELECT DepartmentName FROM EmployeeDepartment WHERE ID = e.DepartmentId)
AS DepartmentName
FROM Employee e
```

Generic performance improvement tips

Here are a couple of pointers to improve the overall application performance in an ASP.NET Core Web Application.

Avoiding the Response.Redirect method

When we want to do client-side redirection, developers can call
the `Response.Redirect` method with the URL passed as a parameter. But there is a small
problem with this approach. If we use `Response.Redirect`, the browser will send the
request to the server again, which needs another round trip to the server. So, if possible, it is
better to avoid the `Response.Redirect` method and instead use
`RedirectToAction` method if possible.

Using string builder

If your application involves a lot of string manipulation, it is preferable to use string builder
instead of the usual string concatenation. String concatenation results in creating a new
string object for each of the operations, whereas string builder works on the single object
itself. We can achieve significantly better performance when we use string builder in large
string manipulation operations.

Summary

In this chapter, we have learned how to analyze the performance of web applications and
which layers to target when improving the performance. Then we discussed how to
improve the performance in each of the layers—the UI layer, the web/application layer, and
the DB layer.

12

ASP.NET Core Identity

Security is essential to all types of applications, including web applications. Would you use Facebook if anyone could update your status by impersonating you? If that were possible, then no one would come back to Facebook. From this example, we can see that security is not so much a feature as it is a necessity for all applications.

In this chapter, we are going to learn about the following topics:

- Authentication and authorization
- ASP.NET Identity
- How to implement security in an ASP.NET Core application using ASP.NET Identity with Entity Framework

When we talk about the security of an application, we primarily want to prevent any unauthorized access, meaning that only the people who have access to the information should be able to access it—nothing more, nothing less.

Before proceeding further, I would like to clarify some of the core concepts regarding security.

Authentication

Authentication is the process of validating whether the user has access to the system. In any application, users will be authenticated first. This can be achieved by asking the user to enter their user ID and password.

Authorization

Authorization is the process where we verify whether the user has access to the requested resource. They might have legitimate access to the system, but they might not have access to the requested resource as they do not have the required access. For example, only the admin user can access the configuration page of the application, whereas normal users should not be allowed to use this page.

ASP.NET Identity provides several features for securing the application.

Let us consider the following simple scenario where the user tries to access the **Secure Page**, a page to which only authorized people should have access. As the user is not logged in, they will be redirected to the **Login Page** so that we can authenticate and authorize the user. Upon successful authentication, the user is redirected to the **Secure Page**. If for any reason, we can not authenticate and authorize the user, we can redirect them to the **"Access denied" Page**:

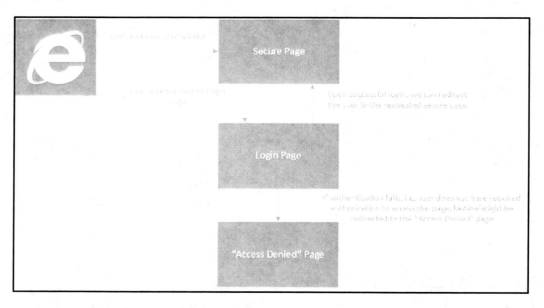

ASP.NET Core Identity is a membership system that enables you to secure the application easily, and which has features such as adding login functionality to your application. The following are the steps that we need to follow in order to use **ASP.NET Identity** (with Entity Framework) for our application:

1. Add the relevant dependencies to the `project.json` file.
2. Create an `appsettings.json` file and store the database connection string.
3. Create an `ApplicationUser` class and `ApplicationDbContext` class.
4. Configure the application to use ASP.NET Identity.
5. Create ViewModels for registration and login.
6. Create the necessary controller and associated action methods and Views.

Adding the relevant dependencies to the project.json file

If you want to use ASP.NET Identity with Entity Framework in your application, you need to add the following dependencies:

```
"EntityFramework.Commands": "7.0.0-rc1-final",
    "EntityFramework.MicrosoftSqlServer": "7.0.0-rc1-final",
    "Microsoft.AspNet.Authentication.Cookies": "1.0.0-rc1-final",
```

Create an `appsettings.json` file and store the database connection string.

Create a file with the name `appsettings.json` at the root level of the project, as shown in the following screenshot:

Store the following connection string in `appsettings.json`. This connection string will be used by ASP.NET Identity to store the data in relevant tables:

```
{
  "Data": {
    "DefaultConnection": {
      "ConnectionString":
"Server=(localdb)\\mssqllocaldb;Database=aspnet_security;Trusted_Connection
=True;MultipleActiveResultSets=true"
```

```
        }
      }
    }
```

Adding ApplicationUser and ApplicationDbContext classes

Create a **Models** folder and a couple of files—**ApplicationDbContext.cs** and**ApplicationUser.cs**—as shown in the following screenshot:

The `ApplicationUser` class inherits from the `IdentityUser` class (available at the `AspNet.Identity.EntityFramework6` namespace) as follows:

```
    public class ApplicationUser : IdentityUser
    {
    ..
    }
```

You can add properties to the user as per the needs of your application. I have not added any properties as I would like to keep things simple to show the features of ASP.NET Identity.

The `ApplicationDbContext` class inherits from the `IdentityDbContext` class of `ApplicationUser`. In the constructor method, we pass the `connectionstring`, which is eventually passed to the base class.

Even the `OnModelCreating` method is overridden. If you want to change any table names (to be generated by Identity), you can do so as follows:

```
    public class ApplicationDbContext : IdentityDbContext<ApplicationUser>
        {
            public ApplicationDbContext(string nameOrConnectionString) :
    base(nameOrConnectionString) { }

            protected override void OnModelCreating(DbModelBuilder
    modelBuilder)
            {
```

```
        base.OnModelCreating(modelBuilder);
    }
}
```

Once we create the `Models` file, we need to configure the application and services. You can configure these in `Configure` and `ConfigureServices`, which are found in the `Startup` class.

Configuring the application to use Identity

In order to use Identity, we just need to add the following line in the `Configure` method of the `Startup` class:

```
app.UseIdentity();
```

The complete `Configure` method is shown in the following code, along with the call of the `UseIdentity` method, which is `app.UseIdentity()`:

```
public void Configure(IApplicationBuilder app, IHostingEnvironment env,
ILoggerFactory loggerFactory)
        {
            loggerFactory.AddConsole(Configuration.GetSection("Logging"));
            loggerFactory.AddDebug();

            if (env.IsDevelopment())
            {
                app.UseBrowserLink();
                app.UseDeveloperExceptionPage();
                app.UseDatabaseErrorPage();
            }
            else
            {
                app.UseExceptionHandler("/Home/Error");


            app.UseIISPlatformHandler(options =>
options.AuthenticationDescriptions.Clear());

            app.UseStaticFiles();

            app.UseIdentity();

            // To configure external authentication please see
        http://go.microsoft.com/fwlink/?LinkID=532715
```

```
app.UseMvc(routes =>
{
    routes.MapRoute(
        name: "default",
        template: "{controller=Home}/{action=Index}/{id?}");
});
}
```

In the `ConfigureServices` method, we will make the following changes:

- We will add the `ApplicationDbContext` class with the connection string taken from the `appsettings.json` file
- We will add Identity with `UserStore` and `RoleStore`
- Finally, we will ask ASP.NET Core to return `AuthMessageSender` whenever we ask for the `IEmailSender` and `ISMSSender` classes

```
public void ConfigureServices(IServiceCollection services
{
// Add framework services.

    services.AddScoped<ApplicationDbContext>(f => {
        return new
ApplicationDbContext(Configuration["Data:DefaultConnection:ConnectionString
"]);
    });
    services.AddIdentity<ApplicationUser, IdentityRole>()
        .AddUserStore<UserStore<ApplicationUser,
ApplicationDbContext>>()
        .AddRoleStore<RoleStore<ApplicationDbContext>>()
        .AddDefaultTokenProviders();

    services.AddMvc();

    // Add application services.
    services.AddTransient<IEmailSender, AuthMessageSender>();
    services.AddTransient<ISmsSender, AuthMessageSender>();
}
```

Creating ViewModels

Next, we will be creating several ViewModels that we will be using in our Views model.

To start with, we will create a `RegisterViewModel` class that contains three properties—`Email`, `Password`, and `ConfirmPassword`. We decorate the properties with appropriate attributes so that we can use client-side validation using an unobtrusive jQuery validation. We are making all the fields required as follows:

```
public class RegisterViewModel
    {
        [Required]
        [EmailAddress]
        [Display(Name = "Email")]
        public string Email { get; set; }

        [Required]
        [StringLength(100, ErrorMessage = "The {0} must be at least {2}
characters long.", MinimumLength = 6)]
        [DataType(DataType.Password)]
        [Display(Name = "Password")]
        public string Password { get; set; }

        [DataType(DataType.Password)]
        [Display(Name = "Confirm password")]
        [Compare("Password", ErrorMessage = "The password and confirmation
password do not match.")]
        public string ConfirmPassword { get; set; }
    }
```

Now, we can create the `LoginViewModel` model, which the user can use to log in to your application. There is an additional property, `RememberMe`, which, when checked, will enable you to log in without having to enter the password again:

```
public class LoginViewModel
    {
        [Required]
        [EmailAddress]
        public string Email { get; set; }

        [Required]
        [DataType(DataType.Password)]
        public string Password { get; set; }

        [Display(Name = "Remember me?")]
        public bool RememberMe { get; set; }
    }
```

Creating Controllers and associated action methods

Now we need to create an `AccountController` class, where we will define the action methods for authentication and authorization:

```
public class AccountController : Controller
    {
        private readonly UserManager<ApplicationUser> _userManager;
        private readonly SignInManager<ApplicationUser> _signInManager;
        private readonly IEmailSender _emailSender;
        private readonly ISmsSender _smsSender;
        private readonly ILogger _logger;

        public AccountController(
            UserManager<ApplicationUser> userManager,
            SignInManager<ApplicationUser> signInManager,
            IEmailSender emailSender,
            ISmsSender smsSender,
            ILoggerFactory loggerFactory)
        {
            _userManager = userManager;
            _signInManager = signInManager;
            _emailSender = emailSender;
            _smsSender = smsSender;
            _logger = loggerFactory.CreateLogger<AccountController>();
        }
    }
```

In the preceding code, we are using services provided by different components. `UserManager` and `SignInManager` are provided by ASP.NET Identity. The `IEmailSender` and `ISmsSender` are custom classes that we have written which will be used for sending e-mails and SMS messages. We will look more at e-mail and SMS later in this chapter. Logging is provided by the Microsoft Logging extension. The following is a simple login `HTTPGET` method. It simply stores the URL from where the `Login` method is accessed and returns the login page:

```
[HttpGet]
        [AllowAnonymous]
        public IActionResult Login(string returnUrl = null)
        {
            ViewData["ReturnUrl"] = returnUrl;
            return View();
        }
```

Creating Views

Now, we will create respective View page for the login. In this View page, we are just showing the following details:

```
@using System.Collections.Generic
@using Microsoft.AspNet.Http
@using Microsoft.AspNet.Http.Authentication
@using AspNet.Identity.EntityFramework6

@model LoginViewModel
@inject SignInManager<ApplicationUser> SignInManager

@{
    ViewData["Title"] = "Log in";
}

<h2>@ViewData["Title"].</h2>
<div class="row">
    <div class="col-md-8">
        <section>
            <form asp-controller="Account" asp-action="Login" asp-route-
returnurl="@ViewData["ReturnUrl"]" method="post" class="form-horizontal"
role="form">
                <h4>Use a local account to log in.</h4>
                <hr />
                <div asp-validation-summary="ValidationSummary.All"
class="text-danger"></div>
                <div class="form-group">
                    <label asp-for="Email" class="col-md-2 control-
label"></label>
                    <div class="col-md-10">
                        <input asp-for="Email" class="form-control" />
                        <span asp-validation-for="Email" class="text-
danger"></span>
                    </div>
                </div>
                <div class="form-group">
                    <label asp-for="Password" class="col-md-2 control-
label"></label>
                    <div class="col-md-10">
                        <input asp-for="Password" class="form-control" />
                        <span asp-validation-for="Password" class="text-
danger"></span>
                    </div>
                </div>
                <div class="form-group">
```

```html
                    <div class="col-md-offset-2 col-md-10">
                        <div class="checkbox">
                            <input asp-for="RememberMe" />
                            <label asp-for="RememberMe"></label>
                        </div>
                    </div>
                </div>
                <div class="form-group">
                    <div class="col-md-offset-2 col-md-10">
                        <button type="submit" class="btn btn-default">Log
in</button>
                    </div>
                </div>
                <p>
                    <a asp-action="Register">Register as a new user?</a>
                </p>
                <p>
                    <a asp-action="ForgotPassword">Forgot your
password?</a>
                </p>
            </form>
        </section>
    </div>
</div>

@section Scripts {
    @{ await Html.RenderPartialAsync("_ValidationScriptsPartial"); }
}
```

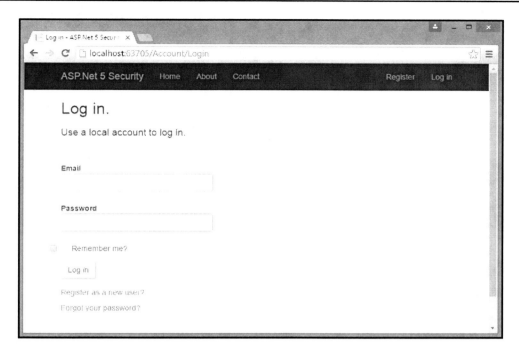

When the user logs into the application for the first time, they might not have any login credentials, so our application should provide a feature that they can use to create a login for themselves. We will create a simple `Register` action method that will just return a View with which the user can register themselves:

```
[HttpGet]
[AllowAnonymous]
public IActionResult Register()
{
    return View();
}
```

We will also create the corresponding View that contains input controls for e-mail, password, password confirmation, and a `Register` button:

```
@model RegisterViewModel
@{
    ViewData["Title"] = "Register";
}

<h2>@ViewData["Title"].</h2>

<form asp-controller="Account" asp-action="Register" method="post"
```

```
class="form-horizontal" role="form">
    <h4>Create a new account.</h4>
    <hr />
    <div asp-validation-summary="ValidationSummary.All" class="text-
danger"></div>
    <div class="form-group">
        <label asp-for="Email" class="col-md-2 control-label"></label>
        <div class="col-md-10">
            <input asp-for="Email" class="form-control" />
            <span asp-validation-for="Email" class="text-danger"></span>
        </div>
    </div>
    <div class="form-group">
        <label asp-for="Password" class="col-md-2 control-label"></label>
        <div class="col-md-10">
            <input asp-for="Password" class="form-control" />
            <span asp-validation-for="Password" class="text-danger"></span>
        </div>
    </div>
    <div class="form-group">
        <label asp-for="ConfirmPassword" class="col-md-2 control-
label"></label>
        <div class="col-md-10">
            <input asp-for="ConfirmPassword" class="form-control" />
            <span asp-validation-for="ConfirmPassword" class="text-
danger"></span>
        </div>
    </div>
    <div class="form-group">
        <div class="col-md-offset-2 col-md-10">
            <button type="submit" class="btn btn-default">Register</button>
        </div>
    </div>
</form>

@section Scripts {
    @{ await Html.RenderPartialAsync("_ValidationScriptsPartial"); }
}
```

The following is the corresponding POST action method for registration. Here, the program checks whether the model is valid, and, if it is valid, it will create an ApplicationUser object using the model data and call the Identity API (the CreateAsync method). If it can create the user variable, the user will log in using that user ID and be redirected to the Home page:

```
[HttpPost]
        [AllowAnonymous]
```

```
      [ValidateAntiForgeryToken]
      public async Task<IActionResult> Register(RegisterViewModel model)
      {
          if (ModelState.IsValid)
          {
              var user = new ApplicationUser { UserName = model.Email,
Email = model.Email };
              var result = await _userManager.CreateAsync(user,
model.Password);
              if (result.Succeeded)
              {
                  await _signInManager.SignInAsync(user, isPersistent:
false);
                  return RedirectToAction(nameof(HomeController.Index),
"Home");
              }
              AddErrors(result);
          }
          return View(model);
      }
```

The log-out functionality is pretty simple. It just needs to call the `SignoutAsync` method of Identity API and be redirected to the `Index` page:

```
[HttpPost]
      [ValidateAntiForgeryToken]
      public async Task<IActionResult> LogOff()
      {
          await _signInManager.SignOutAsync();
          _logger.LogInformation(4, "User logged out.");
          return RedirectToAction(nameof(HomeController.Index), "Home");
      }
```

Coming back to the log-in functionality, the following is the respective action method. We are calling the `PasswordSignInAsync` method of Identity API. Upon a successful login, we redirect the URL from where the log-in functionality is accessed:

```
[HttpPost]
      [AllowAnonymous]
      [ValidateAntiForgeryToken]
      public async Task<IActionResult> Login(LoginViewModel model, string
returnUrl = null)
      {
          ViewData["ReturnUrl"] = returnUrl;
          if (ModelState.IsValid)
          {
              var result = await
_signInManager.PasswordSignInAsync(model.Email, model.Password,
```

```
model.RememberMe, lockoutOnFailure: false);
            if (result.Succeeded)
            {
                return RedirectToLocal(returnUrl);
            }
        }
        // If there is any error, display the form again
        return View(model);
    }
```

E-mail and SMS services

If you want to add e-mail and SMS services to your application's authentication capabilities, you can do so by creating the interfaces and classes shown here:

```
public interface IEmailSender
{
    Task SendEmailAsync(string email, string subject, string message)
}
  public interface ISmsSender
    {
    Task SendSmsAsync(string number, string message);
    }
public class AuthMessageSender : IEmailSender, ISmsSender
    {
    public Task SendEmailAsync(string email, string subject, string
message)
    {
        // We can plug in our email service here to send an email.
        return Task.FromResult(0);
    }
    public Task SendSmsAsync(string number, string message)
    {
        // We can plug in our SMS service here to send a text message.
        return Task.FromResult(0);
    }
    }
```

Securing an action method in a Controller

For the sake of explanation, let us assume that the **About** page is a secure page and only authenticated users should be able to access it.

We just have to decorate the `About` action method in the `Home` controller with an `[Authorize]` attribute:

```
[Authorize]
        public IActionResult About()
        {
            ViewData["Message"] = "This is my about page";
            return View();
        }
```

Making the preceding change will redirect the user to the log-in page when the user tries to access the log-in page without logging in to the application:

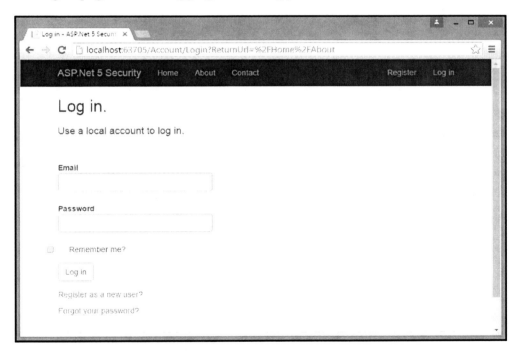

In the following screenshot, you will notice an additional query parameter, `ReturnURL`, in the URL. This `ReturnURL` parameter will redirect the application to that specific page (the value passed in the `ReturnURL` parameter—**Home/About** in our case).

Once you log in, you'll be redirected to the page that you requested earlier:

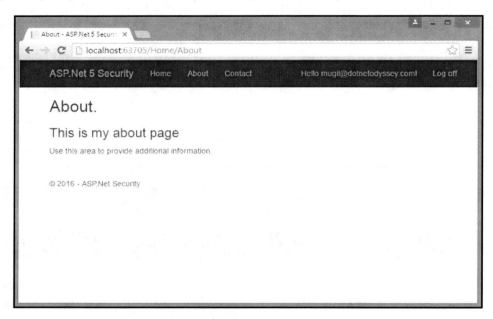

When you register a new user, the details of the user will be stored in the relevant tables created by ASP.NET Identity.

Open the SQL Server Object Explorer window by selecting the option **View | SQL Server Object Explorer**, as shown in the following screenshot:

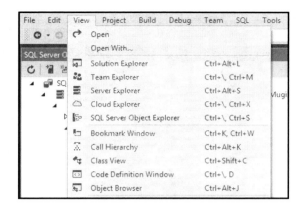

Once you select the **SQL Server Object Explorer** option, you will see a window similar to the following screenshot. ASP.NET Identity creates a database for us by using Entity Framework and the connection string that we provided earlier in the `appsettings.json` package.

ASP.NET Identity creates several tables to maintain identity-related information and the database migration history of Entity Framework. As we are using ASP.NET Identity at the basic level, none of the identity-related tables will get populated, apart from **dbo.AspNetUsers.**:

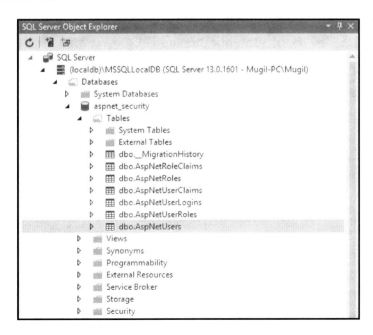

You can right-click on the **dbo.AspNetUsers** table and select **View Data** to see the data:

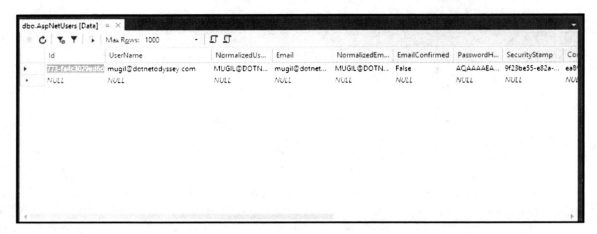

As only one user has been registered in our application, only one row has been created. Please note that the hashed password (marked by ASP.NET Identity for us) and no blank passwords will get stored in the table.

Summary

In this chapter, we learned about authentication and authorization. We also learned how to implement ASP.NET Identity in an ASP.NET Core application by following a step-by-step process. We also discussed the tables involved in ASP.NET Identity and learned how to see the data created by ASP.NET Identity.

Index